First World War
and Army of Occupation
War Diary
France, Belgium and Germany

17 DIVISION
Headquarters, Branches and Services
Royal Army Ordnance Corps
Deputy Assistant Director Ordnance Services
14 July 1915 - 12 February 1919

WO95/1990/2

The Naval & Military Press Ltd
www.nmarchive.com
Published in association with The National Archives

Published by

The Naval & Military Press Ltd

Unit 10 Ridgewood Industrial Park,

Uckfield, East Sussex,

TN22 5QE England

Tel: +44 (0) 1825 749494

www.naval-military-press.com

www.nmarchive.com

This diary has been reprinted in facsimile from the original. Any imperfections are inevitably reproduced and the quality may fall short of modern type and cartographic standards.

© **Crown Copyright**
Images reproduced by permission of The National Archives, London, England, 2015.

Contents

Document type	Place/Title	Date From	Date To
Heading	WO95/1990/2		
Heading	17th Division D.A.D.O.S. Jly 1915-Feb 1919		
Heading	17th Division Hd: Qrs 17th Div. D.A.D.O.S. Vol:I 121/6753 Jly To Aug. 15		
Heading	Confidential War Diary Of D.A.D.O.S. XVII Division From 1st July 1915 To 31st August 1915		
War Diary	Lombre	14/07/1915	17/07/1915
War Diary	March To Renescure	18/07/1915	18/07/1915
War Diary	March To Steenvorde	19/07/1915	24/07/1915
War Diary	Reninghelst	25/07/1915	31/08/1915
Heading	17th Division H.Q. 17th Division D.A.D.O.S. Vol. II 121/6923 Sept. 15		
Heading	War Diary Of D.A.D.O.S. 17th Division From 1st September 1915 to 30th September 1915		
War Diary	Reninghelst	01/09/1915	30/09/1915
Operation(al) Order(s)	Divisional Routine Order No 57	12/09/1915	12/09/1915
Heading	121/7592 H.Q. 17th Div. D.A.D.O.S. Vol 3 Oct 15		
Heading	Confidential War Diary of D.A.D.O.S. 17th Division From 1st Oct 1915 to 31st October 1915 Volume 3		
War Diary	Reninghelst	01/10/1915	06/10/1915
War Diary	Steenvoorde	08/10/1915	21/10/1915
War Diary	Reninghelst	22/10/1915	31/10/1915
Heading	H.Q. 17th Div. D.A.D.O.S. Vol 4 121/7624 Nov 15		
Heading	Confidential War Diary of D A D O S 17th Division From 1st November 1915 to 30th November 1915		
War Diary	Reninghelst	01/11/1915	30/11/1915
Heading	D.A.D.O.S. 17th Div. Vol.5 121/7928		
War Diary	Reninghelst	02/12/1915	31/12/1915
Heading	D.A.D.O.S. 17th Div. Vol 6 Jan. 1916		
War Diary	Reninghelst	01/01/1916	06/01/1916
War Diary	Moulle	07/01/1916	06/02/1916
War Diary	Reninghelst	07/02/1916	29/02/1916
Heading	D.A.D.O.S. 17 Div. Vol 8		
War Diary	Reninghelst	01/03/1916	07/03/1916
War Diary	Steenvoorde	08/03/1916	09/03/1916
War Diary	Merris	10/03/1916	21/03/1916
War Diary	P.de Nieppe	22/03/1916	31/03/1916
Miscellaneous	D.A.G. 3rd Echelon Base		
War Diary	Pont de Nieppe	01/04/1916	14/05/1916
War Diary	Tilques	15/05/1916	09/06/1916
War Diary	Heilly	10/06/1916	10/06/1916
War Diary	Allonville	11/06/1916	27/06/1916
War Diary	Mericourt Le Abbe	28/06/1916	09/07/1916
War Diary	Cavillon	10/07/1916	14/07/1916
War Diary	Pont Remy Somme	15/07/1916	22/07/1916
War Diary	Ribemont	23/07/1916	01/08/1916
War Diary	E10.B 0.1 Sheet 67.D Near Albert	02/08/1916	06/08/1916
War Diary	Field Depot E.10.B 7.9 Near Albert	07/08/1916	12/08/1916
War Diary	Ribemont and Somme	13/08/1916	15/08/1916
War Diary	Bernaville	16/08/1916	16/08/1916

War Diary	Doullens	17/08/1916	20/08/1916
War Diary	Henn	21/08/1916	26/08/1916
Heading	War Diary Of Dados 17th Div For Sept. 1916 Vol.14		
War Diary	Henn	03/09/1916	21/09/1916
War Diary	St Riquier	22/09/1916	30/09/1916
Heading	Confidential War Diary Of D A D O S 17th Division October 1916 Vol 15		
War Diary	St Riquier	01/10/1916	05/10/1916
War Diary	Pas	06/10/1916	21/10/1916
War Diary	Treux	22/10/1916	25/10/1916
War Diary	Citadel N James	26/10/1916	31/10/1916
Heading	War Diary Of D A D O S 17th Division Nov:1916 Vol 16		
War Diary	Minder Post	01/11/1916	09/11/1916
War Diary	Mericourt L. Abbe	11/11/1916	14/11/1916
War Diary	Oissy	15/11/1916	12/12/1916
War Diary	Corbie	13/12/1916	24/12/1916
War Diary	Plateau	25/12/1916	25/12/1916
War Diary	Minden Post	27/12/1916	31/12/1916
Heading	War Diary For Jan. 1917	31/01/1917	31/01/1917
War Diary	Plateau	01/01/1917	13/01/1917
War Diary	Mericourt	14/01/1917	25/01/1917
War Diary	Plateau	27/01/1917	31/01/1917
Heading	War Diary Of D.A.D.O.S. 17th Division For February 1917 Vol 19		
War Diary	Plateau	01/02/1917	16/02/1917
War Diary	Grovetown	17/02/1917	17/02/1917
War Diary	Plateau	18/02/1917	18/02/1917
War Diary	Mericourt	19/02/1917	01/03/1917
War Diary	Varennes	03/03/1917	10/03/1917
War Diary	Auxi-Le-Chateau	15/03/1917	16/03/1917
War Diary	Bouquemaison	21/03/1917	30/03/1917
War Diary	Le Cauroy	02/04/1917	07/04/1917
War Diary	Berneville	08/04/1917	15/04/1917
War Diary	Arras	16/04/1917	30/04/1917
War Diary	Le Cauroy	01/05/1917	06/05/1917
War Diary	Arras	11/05/1917	31/05/1917
War Diary	Couturelle	01/06/1917	18/06/1917
War Diary	St Nicolas	23/06/1917	24/09/1917
War Diary	Le Cauroy	26/09/1917	04/10/1917
War Diary	Proven	05/10/1917	12/10/1917
War Diary	Elverdinghe	13/10/1917	20/10/1917
War Diary	Zutkerque	23/10/1917	05/11/1917
War Diary	Elverdinghe	08/11/1917	08/12/1917
War Diary	Zutkerque	11/12/1917	14/12/1917
War Diary	Achiet-Le-petit	19/12/1917	19/12/1917
War Diary	Bealencourt	20/12/1917	24/12/1917
War Diary	Bus	25/12/1917	24/02/1918
War Diary	Bertincourt	26/02/1918	21/03/1918
War Diary	Beaulencourt	22/03/1918	23/03/1918
War Diary	Courcelette	24/03/1918	24/03/1918
War Diary	Henencourt	25/03/1917	25/03/1917
War Diary	Vardencourt	26/03/1918	26/03/1918
War Diary	Puchevillers	27/03/1918	29/03/1918
War Diary	Mirvaux	30/03/1918	31/03/1918
War Diary	Pierregot	03/04/1918	04/04/1918

War Diary	Havernas	05/04/1918	12/04/1918
War Diary	Halloy	15/04/1918	29/04/1918
War Diary	Halloy-L-Pernois	02/05/1918	19/05/1918
War Diary	Raincheval	25/05/1918	13/08/1918
War Diary	Laneuville	15/08/1918	18/08/1918
War Diary	Puchevillers	19/08/1918	27/08/1918
War Diary	Englebelmer	28/08/1918	03/09/1918
War Diary	Martinpuich	06/09/1918	07/09/1918
War Diary	Le Transloy	08/09/1918	30/09/1918
War Diary	Fins	01/10/1918	12/10/1918
War Diary	Montigny	14/10/1918	22/10/1918
War Diary	Inchy	25/10/1918	05/11/1918
War Diary	Poix-Du-Nord	06/11/1918	07/11/1918
War Diary	Locquignol	09/11/1918	12/11/1918
War Diary	Inchy	13/11/1918	10/12/1918
War Diary	Hallencourt	10/12/1918	12/02/1919

Elogiola

17TH DIVISION

D. A. D. O. S.
JLY 1915 – FEB 1919

D/6753

Deas

14th/15 Warrw

H.O. Cos. 17th Div: S.A.S.O.
Vol: I

Jy 8 & Aug 15

CONFIDENTIAL

War Diary
of
DADOS XVII Division

From 1st July 1915   To 31st August 1915

(Volume 1.)   (Major H Lovett
                       ADOS)

WAR DIARY
or
INTELLIGENCE SUMMARY
(Erase heading not required.)

Army Form C. 2118

DADS 17th Division
July 1915

Place	Date	Hour	Summary of Events and Information	Remarks and references to Appendices
LUMBRES	1915 14/7	2 pm	Arrived from England with Head Quarters of the 17th Divn via St Omer. Having previously reported to D.D.o.S G.H.Q. D¼ Maj⁺	
do	15/7	8 pm	Attended at Rail Head to make arrangements for Stores arriving D¼ Maj⁺	
do	16/7	9 pm	Interviewed D.D.o.S regarding W.Het carts &c to c advised O.C. 51st Fd Ambce regarding repair of Wagons Other Routine Work. Took over an empty House as Offices – It is situated near the Post Office – D¼ Maj⁺	
do	17/7	5 pm	To St Omer Railhead – Home to camp of Mtd Bgde arranged for an office. It is situated near the Post Office – D¼ Maj⁺ To St Omer Railhead to reconnoitre next Rail Head – D¼ Maj⁺ Smoke Helmets – D¼ Maj⁺	
RENESCURE	18/7	6 pm	Rested one night. D¼ Maj⁺	
March to STEENVOORDE 19/7 to 24/7	19/7	6 pm	Opened Smoke Office D¼ Maj⁺ Distributed Smoke Helmets – N.O. Dump established D¼ Maj⁺	
RENINGHELST			established a Temporary Dump. D¼ Maj⁺	

WAR DIARY
INTELLIGENCE SUMMARY
(Erase heading not required.)

Army Form C. 2118

SA ADS/17th July 1915

Instructions regarding War Diaries and Intelligence Summaries are contained in F.S. Regs., Part II. and the Staff Manual respectively. Title Pages will be prepared in manuscript.

Place	Date 1915	Hour	Summary of Events and Information	Remarks and references to Appendices
REMINGHELST	26/7	6pm	Routine work only. S/Maj'r	
	27/7	5pm	" " — Inspector of Horse Transport asked me to obtain a large no. of Horse Shoes, referred question to DDVS 2nd Army, these were supplied. S/Maj'r	
	28/7	5pm	Routine work. S/Maj'r	
	29/7	5pm	Routine work. S/Maj'r	
	30/7	5:30p	Routine work. S/Maj'r	
	31/7	5:30p	Routine work — Shortage of Spares for LEWIS machine guns referred to Ordnance 2nd Army. S/Maj'r	

Army Form C. 2118

DADVS 17th Divn

WAR DIARY

INTELLIGENCE SUMMARY

August 1915

(Erase heading not required.)

Instructions regarding War Diaries and Intelligence Summaries are contained in F. S. Regs., Part II. and the Staff Manual respectively. Title Pages will be prepared in manuscript.

Place	Date	Hour	Summary of Events and Information	Remarks and references to Appendices
REMINGHELST	1st	7pm	Routine Work. JV Maj'r	
	2nd	6pm	Routine Work JV Maj'n	
	3rd	6pm	Rail head at "HAZEBROUCK GARAGE" JV Maj'r	
	4"	7pm	2 Lewis machine guns issued this date, completes each batn with 4. Routine duties JV Maj'r	
	5"	6pm	Routine Work JV Maj'r	
	6"	1p	Routine Work JV Maj'r	
	7	5.30p	Routine Work JV Maj'r	
	8"	5.50pm	Routine Work JV Maj'r	
	9"	6pm	Routine Work JV Maj'r	
	10"	5.45p	Routine Work JV Maj'r	
	11"	6pm	Routine Work JV Maj'r	
	12"	5.5pm	Routine Work - First receipt of Tube Helmets - to issue to Machine Gunners JV Maj'r	
	13	6pm	Routine Work. Received percentage of Smoke Helmets for Horses JV Maj'r	
	14	7pm	Routine Work Transferred 500 Tube for Smoke Helmets to S Divn JV Maj'r	

Army Form C. 2118

WAR DIARY D.A.D.O.S. XIII Dn

INTELLIGENCE SUMMARY August 1915

(Erase heading not required.)

Instructions regarding War Diaries and Intelligence Summaries are contained in F. S. Regs., Part II. and the Staff Manual respectively. Title Pages will be prepared in manuscript.

Place	Date	Hour	Summary of Events and Information	Remarks and references to Appendices
RENING HELST	15th	6pm	Routine Work - H major	
	16'	6pm	Routine Work H major	
	17'	6pm	Routine Work H major	
	18	6.15pm	Routine Work - A Bg 81st Bde RFA (How) Transferred Canadian Div. H major	
	19	5.15	Routine work. H major	
	20	6pm	Routine work - Read 2 loan from to replace "U" H major	
	21	5.55pm	Routine Work - Read Two Helmets for Officers + NCOs H major	
	22	6.30pm	Routine Work. Orders to hand in 500 Tube helmets to 1st Div. accompanied these was held up when nearing "POPERINGE" owing to heavy fire. 2 Shells burst very near Motor Lorry + Car. H major	
	23	5.30pm	Routine Work H major	
	24	6pm	Routine Work - Orders Received to transfer 1600 Tube Helmets to 3rd Division H major	
	25	6.15pm	Routine Work H major	
	26	6pm	Routine Work H major	

WAR DIARY

INTELLIGENCE SUMMARY

ADOS 17' Div

August 1915

Army Form C. 2118

Place	Date	Hour	Summary of Events and Information	Remarks and references to Appendices
REMINGHELST	27	7a	Routine Work H Major	
	28	6pm	Routine Work H Major	
	29	6pm	Routine Work H Major	
	30	4pm	Routine Work H Major	
	31	5.30p	Routine Work H Major	

Howell Myers
D.a.D.S. 17 Div

121/6923

17th Division

H.Q. 17th Division S.A.O.S.
Vol: II

Sept 15

Confidential

War Diary

of

DADOS 17th Division

From 1st September 1915 to 30th September 1915

(Volume XII)

(Major H Lovett)
AOD

Army Form C. 2118

WAR DIARY ~~INTELLIGENCE SUMMARY~~

DADS XII Div September 1915

(Erase heading not required.)

Instructions regarding War Diaries and Intelligence Summaries are contained in F.S. Regs., Part II. and the Staff Manual respectively. Title Pages will be prepared in manuscript.

Place	Date	Hour	Summary of Events and Information	Remarks and references to Appendices
RENINGHELST	1st	9pm	Routine Work. J/Maj"	
	2"	6.15p	Routine Work. J/Maj"	
	3"	6 pm	Routine Work J/Maj"	
	4"	6 pm	Routine Work - Advice of 5000 blankets allotted - cancelled. Recd 4,500 blankets from 4 Divr. J/Maj.	
	5"	5.50p	Routine Work - J/Maj"	
	6	5.45p	Routine Work J/Maj	
	7"	5.50p	Routine Work J/Maj"	

Army Form C. 2118

DADOS XVII Div WAR DIARY or INTELLIGENCE SUMMARY September 1915

Place	Date	Hour	Summary of Events and Information	Remarks and references to Appendices
RENINGHELST	8th	5 p	Routine work – 17th Divl Sub Park. the administrator by DADOS	
			5th Corps ordnance officer	
	9th	6 p	Routine work. Rail head changed to "GODEWAERSVELDE" 24 mm	
	10th	5.30p	Routine Work – 9000 Tube helmets Recd also 100 C.S.L. tents. 3 mmy	
	11th	7 p	" – 9.30 do – as part of 51,865 of Equipt. to Divn	
			Attended 15th – 1 Administrative Officers at-	
			"Q" Office – Requested to try tools to enable units to	
			Construct "Bivouacs". Large proportion of tube helmets issued 3 mmy	
	12th	6.45p	Routine duties. All tube helmets havg been Recd & Isd	"1"
			Routine order was published – DA Major	
	13th	7.30p	Routine Work – One Lewis gun demanded to replace "V" with 12" barrels	
	14th	6.40p	Routine work – DA major	
	15th	6.15p	– " – DA Major	
	16th	6 p	– do – DA major	

WAR DIARY *or* INTELLIGENCE SUMMARY

DADOS XVII Div

Army Form C. 2118

September 1915

(Erase heading not required.)

Place	Date	Hour	Summary of Events and Information	Remarks and references to Appendices
	17th	7.10 pm	Routine work DA major	
	18th	6.15 pm	— do — DA major	
	19th	6.5 pm	— do — DA major	
	20th	6.20 pm	— do — DA major	
	21st	6.50 pm	— do — Conference over AA&QMG hqs to discuss points in Div M. Connection with army move forward DA major	
	22nd	11.10 pm	Routine Work DA major	
	23rd	5 pm	Routine work — DL major DA maj.	
	24th	7 pm	Routine work	
	25th	7.10 pm	Routine Work — 1st Consignment of Satchels for Tube helmets rec'd Routine work DA	
	26	5 pm	Rec'd 36. Saloon breathing apparatus DA	
	27	5-15 pm	Work — Satchels rec'd in full DA	
	28	6 pm	Routine work — 36 Saloon breathing apparatus issued to troops DA	
	29	5 pm	Routine work DA	
	30	6.30 pm	Routine work — DA	

Howell Major
DADOS 17 Div
30-9-1915-

No "1"

Divisional Routine Order N° 57
by
M.Genl T D Pilcher CB Comdg 17 Dn
12 Sept 1915

N° 253 Smoke helmets & Respirator

Smoke helmets will be held by R.A., R.E., Infantry, M.M. Gun Battery, & R.A.m.c (including A.S.C personnel attached to Field Ambulances).

Each Officer & man should carry one tube helmet & one film helmet.

One film helmet per officer & man is held in A.O.D. Reserve.

The helmets are available & should be issued forthwith.

The surplus film pattern helmet and Respirator - including Reserves with units - should be withdrawn at once and returned to D.A.D.O.S. This is to be considered an urgent service.

(Sd) F.C. Muspratt Colonel
AA & QMG 17 Divn

True copy

12/9/15

H Lovett Major
DADOS 17 Dn

121/7592

H.Q. 17th Div: STAFF.
Vol 3
Oct 15

Confidential

War Diary

of

D.A.D.O.S 17th Division

From 1st Oct 1915 to 31st October 1915

Volume # 3

WAR DIARY or **INTELLIGENCE SUMMARY**

D.A.D.O.S. 17th Division Army Form C. 2118

October 1915

Place	Date	Hour	Summary of Events and Information	Remarks and references to Appendices
RENINGHELST	1st	7pm	Routine Work - Advised that 7th Belgian Artillery Regt. is transferred from 46th Divsn.; also that rail head is changed from GODEWAERSVELDE to BAVINCHOVE for one day only. H.Major	
	2nd	7pm	Routine Work - Advised that 2 N.M. Brigade R.F.A is transferred from 46th Divn. Rail head at BAVINCHOVE. H.Major	
	3rd	9pm	Routine Work - Rail head returned to GODEWAERSVELDE. Received outstanding indents and particulars regarding the 7th Belgian Artillery Regt. H.Major	
	4th	6pm	Orders received for Division to evacuate RENINGHELST. Routine Work. H.Major	
	5th	6pm	All "bulk" and "detail" Stores have been issued to troops of the Division. Dump is now ready for incoming D.A.D.O.S. Routine Work H.Major	
	6th	7pm	Rail head transferred to "CASSEL". Moved from RENINGHELST to STEENVOORDE. Took over Dump of 24th Division. Before leaving old Station Divisional Reserve of Sub Helmets were handed over to 24th Divn. H.Major	
	7th	7pm	Routine Work. H.Major	

Army Form C. 2118

WA R DIARY
or
INTELLIGENCE SUMMARY

(Erase heading not required.)

A.D.O.S. 17th Division   October 19/15

Place	Date	Hour	Summary of Events and Information	Remarks and references to Appendices
STEEN-VOORDE	8th	6.30p	Divisional Armourers Shop closed temporarily and armourers returned to their Unit Battalion (whilst at "Rest." Routine Work. JA Major	
	9th	7p	Routine Work – Received 1st Consignment of Winter Clothing 34,000 Drawers from O/c dromonts 17/ for mould men – some complaint regarding the carrying of this 2d pair for the men – proposed that the 2d pair for dismounted men be withdrawn and either stored at Rest Station or disposed of as orders fr DDOS 2d Army – Them forms will be referred accordingly JA Major	
	10th	6.15pm	Routine Work. JA Major	
	11th	6 p	Routine Work – Railhead Changed from CASSEL to CASTRE JA Major	
	12th	6.30p	Routine Work – JA Major	
	13th	6.45p	Routine Work – JA Major	
	14th	5pm	I have found it advantageous to send lorries to railhead as early as possible in the morning – Stores are available earlier + the Dump is cleared more often. JA Major	
	15	6p	Routine Work JA Major	
	16	6.30p	Routine Work JA Major	

Army Form C. 2118

WAR DIARY
or
INTELLIGENCE SUMMARY

(Erase heading not required.)

D.A.D.S. 17 Division

Instructions regarding War Diaries and Intelligence Summaries are contained in F.S. Regs., Part II. and the Staff Manual respectively. Title Pages will be prepared in manuscript.

Place	Date	Hour	Summary of Events and Information	Remarks and references to Appendices
STEENVOORDE	17th to 21st	—	Routine Work at Rest Billets. D.A.D.S. 17th Divn	
REMINGHELST	22nd	6pm	Moved from Rest Billets to French Head Quarters at REMINGHELST.	D.A.D.S. 17 Divn at BAILLEUL A/Major
	23rd	6pm	Railhead changes CASTRE to BAILLEUL A/Major	
	24th	6pm	Routine Work D.A.D.S. 17 Major	
	25th	6pm	Routine Work D.A.D.S. 17 Major	
	26	6pm	Routine Work Lt Maj. Major	
	27	6pm	Routine Work Lt Major	
	28	6pm	Routine Work Lt Maj. D.A.D.S. Major	
	29	6pm	Routine Work Lt Maj. Major	
	30	5.50p	Routine Work D.A.D.S. Major	
	31st	6pm	Routine Work	

H Lovett Major
D.A.D.S. 17 Divn

H.Q. 17th Div:
B.A.O.R.
Folio 4

12/7624

Nov 15.

Confidential
War Diary
of
D.A.D.O.S. 17th Division

From 1st November 1915 to 30th November 1915

Volume 1.

Army Form C. 2118

D.A.D.O.S   17th Division

WAR DIARY
or
INTELLIGENCE SUMMARY
(Erase heading not required.)

Instructions regarding War Diaries and Intelligence Summaries are contained in F.S. Regs., Part II. and the Staff Manual respectively. Title Pages will be prepared in manuscript.

Place	Date	Hour	Summary of Events and Information	Remarks and references to Appendices
RENINGHELST	November 1st	5pm	Railway truck containing tent-bottoms are coming too fast for A.O.D. lorries to clear. Applied to Divl Supply Column for assistance. Unfinished cases not be given. Instructions from 2nd Army on this subject to day. Routine Work. H Major	
	2nd	6pm	Routine Work H Major	
	3"	6pm	Routine Work H Major	
	4th	6pm	Routine Work H Major	
	5"	6pm	Routine Work H Major	
	6"	5pm	do H Major	
	7"	5.20p	do H Major	
	8"	6pm	do H Major	
	9"	5.30p	do H Major	
	10"	5pm	do H Major	
	11"	5pm	Routine Work - Lieut H.G. Weller A.O.D arrived to learn me work of D.D.O. H Major	
	12"	5pm	Routine Work H Major	

WAR DIARY
or
INTELLIGENCE SUMMARY

DADOS   17' Division

Army Form C. 2118

(Erase heading not required.)

Instructions regarding War Diaries and Intelligence Summaries are contained in F.S. Regs., Part II. and the Staff Manual respectively. Title Pages will be prepared in manuscript.

Place	Date	Hour	Summary of Events and Information	Remarks and references to Appendices
RENINGHELST	13	5pm	Routine Work	
	14	4pm	do	
	15	6pm	do	
	16	6.30p	do	
	17	3pm	do	
	18	5pm	do	
	19	5pm	do	
	20	5pm	do	
	21	5pm	do	
	22	5.15pm	do	
	23	5.30p	do	
	24	6pm	do	
	25	5.30pm	do	
	26	5pm	do	
	27	6.15pm	do	
	28	6pm	do	
	30		do	

Army Form C. 2118

WAR DIARY or INTELLIGENCE SUMMARY
(Erase heading not required.)

DADOS 17th Division
December 1915

Instructions regarding War Diaries and Intelligence Summaries are contained in F. S. Regs., Part II. and the Staff Manual respectively. Title Pages will be prepared in manuscript.

Place: Pringhets

Date	Hour	Summary of Events and Information	Remarks and references to Appendices
Dec 1915 1st	5pm	Took over the entries of DADOS. Reports departure of my H. Forrest ADS to England, by invoice posts 2nd Army	
2nd		Recd from my Inver Fer. 1193 A.J. List of Imprest a/c.	
3rd	6pm	Went to Railhead & Bailleul for I.P. Routine work. Had two Armstrong bran covers for L.E. for Imprest a/c	
4	5pm		
5	6/-	Routine work	
6	5pm	Went to Hazebrouck for payment of Moorings. Cheques received from Bailleul & Godewaersvelde notice invoiced.	
7	6/-	Routine work	
8	5pm	Routine work. Went to Commentieres to Armee for the French Commence Trench	
9	7	To Hazebrouck enquiring on to armee of Hammocks for next billets Boots	
10	6pm	Re cutter, price 17 fcs. covered up 6/5 high	
11	5-	Railhead, enquiries made for pairs of Hammocks, for next billets	
12	5pm	Routine work. Invoices to Hazebrouck & Trench Boots	
13	6pm	Routine work	
14	6/-	Interview ADOS set Corps in to procedure	ADOS

r875 Wt. W593/826 1,000,000 4/15 J.B.C. &A. A.D.S.S./Forms/C. 2118.

WAR DIARY
or
INTELLIGENCE SUMMARY

Army Form C. 2118

17th Division

December 1915

Place	Date	Hour	Summary of Events and Information	Remarks and references to Appendices
	15	5 pm	Went to Hazebrouck to see to prepare work. Tried Cook not being up to it.	
	16	7 am	Results nil / nil. Musketry returns.	
			Went to Steenvoorde to K. got full nos supplies. Also R. Eng. certain materials of work done by nonpeople named 2 or shown in respect of	
	17	6½	made up supervision. numbers out of ground cables for men in Rest billets.	
	18	4	Routine work	
	19	4	" "	
			Saw some L Type multi core helios	
	20	6½		
	21	7 am	201 + 3/Pk Bde returns owing to attack ended 11.30 am	
			Went to Bailleul – bayonet purchasing store	
	22	4	Routine work	
	23	4		
			To arrange purchasing Shop camp for Signal purposes	
	24	6½	Routine work	
	25	4	Xmas day. Routine work	
	26	4	Went to undergoing to purchase lamps for Signalling purposes	
			personnel B. Staff camp	
	27			

1875 Wt W593/826 1,000,000 4/15 J.B.C. & A. A.D.S.S./Forms/C. 2118.

WAR DIARY
or
INTELLIGENCE SUMMARY

Army Form C. 2118

17 Division
December 1915

Place	Date	Hour	Summary of Events and Information	Remarks and references to Appendices
	27	5?		
	28	6/		
	29	8h		
	30	6/h		
	31	5/		

Diario 17ᵗʰ Stri.
Vol: 6

Tau 1516

Army Form C. 2118

WAR DIARY
or
INTELLIGENCE SUMMARY
(Erase heading not required.)

17 Armoured Key
January 1915

Instructions regarding War Diaries and Intelligence
Summaries are contained in F. S. Regs., Part II.
and the Staff Manual respectively. Title Pages
will be prepared in manuscript.

Place	Date	Hour	Summary of Events and Information	Remarks and references to Appendices
Rawalpindi	1	5p	To Telegs to find suitable place for Train to Entrain Troops in Red area R	
	2	6p	Routine work. AM	
	3	5p	Fitted up 70 Trucks at Moulla AM	
	4	9pm	Preparing for more unsettled Stores for the day re Railways AM	
	5	5p	First Trucks moved to Moulla AM	
	6	5p	To Canal - new Railhead during entraining. Lorries AM. delays through congestion of traffic & Rlys	
Moulla	7	5pc	Took over Orderan a Trucks at Moulla reports 2 or Brigades AM	
	8	6p	Inspection of Trucks demand 10 trs a day for trammels AM which appear reasonable, have arranged for Transit transport officer to intervene the Inspector to obtain a decision re Trans Lines Officers. own can 3 to 9 trs daily after 12th with walls to be received by trains AM	

WAR DIARY or INTELLIGENCE SUMMARY

Army Form C. 2118

Depot 17 Division January 1916

Place	Date	Hour	Summary of Events and Information	Remarks and references to Appendices
	10	9a	Routine work 17D	
	11	9a	Routine work 17D	
	12	1p	Routine work 17D	
	13	9a	Routine work 17D	
	14	7p	Routine work 17D	
	15		Routine work 17D	
	23		Down on leave to England 17D	
	24	5pm	To Walton R.T.O. reports that train arrangements are quite satisfactory	
	26	6/p	Routine work 17D	
	27	5pm	Routine work 17D	
	28	8pm	Preparation of Pump states that 2 fog huts and a of 7 calendars	
			Line twig spreads in trench situations not covered 17D	
	29	5/p	Routine work 17D	
	30	4p	To Canal to see French periscope 17D	
	31	5/p	Monthly return received, a need orders won 17D	

31/1/16 H.C.Sidwell Lieut
Adjt 17 Div

Army Form C. 2118

WAR DIARY
or
INTELLIGENCE SUMMARY

(Erase heading not required.)

HQ Wessex Divn ADDS 17th Divn February 1916

Place	Date	Hour	Summary of Events and Information	Remarks and references to Appendices
Merville	1	5½	To Hazebrouck purchasing Canvas Rubber most HPW	
"	2	4/½	To DSC to arrange for Lorries to be regularly overhauled — arranged for one to go at a time, whilst in, rest open. Truck 41,006 containing 5 ton general stores including 15 wheels HPW	
"	3	5½	Truck 89375 received 8 ton of general stores including 10 Sprayers Knapsack. HPW	
"	4	4/½	Truck 12,072 also Truck 40055 received general stores. — Tracer gun helmets, have chosen a machine from Lorry for 90 W Reserve. Also new 10 tons to prepare to move dump to Renighurst. Sent Lorry to Calais for supplementing stores no more most collects Both in Tube Helmets.	
"	5	5½	Truck 25028 7.45 genl stores, also 47 cases of P.H. Helmets — for reequipping Divi. also Truck 19149 and 168 cases of P.H. Helmets, going to move recovered Truck 19149 & 47 cases back to Calais; until more too been completed. HPW	

WAR DIARY or INTELLIGENCE SUMMARY

Army Form C. 2118

4th/5th Welsh Field Ambulance
7 pm
February 1916

Place	Date	Hour	Summary of Events and Information	Remarks and references to Appendices
Morval	6.	6/7.	Routine work, preparing to move camp ready for orders to trek to Reninghelst.	
Reninghelst	7	5/7.	Moved to Reninghelst. Took over 3rd Division dump & interchanged some such stores, to prevent wastage. ATD	
"	8	17.	Routine work, fixing up Dump. To trek ATD	
"	9	17.	Major's holiday called, issued to Anzacks for supply dumps for convoys sent to trenches. Trench 75583 5 tons. 130316 4 tons & bgds. Trench 23141 4 tons & 20 cars. F.S. Boots ATD	
"	10	5/7.	Trench 52478 5 tons & 200 Helmets Trench Trench 14681 & various etc. " 90096 82 Cans 1 Helmet Tnch. P.H., white enamel, Dresser of 1 pm offr & man ATD	
"	11		HQrs. V Corps called. Ordered a First Boot repairing shop, also equipment of new cook carry on Belts system on any other work without hitch, & to then interchange all. Key ex 20 Chm, having his experience in all branches of First work Tnch 2 gr 5 tm & 40 knapsack sprayers ATD	

WAR DIARY
or
INTELLIGENCE SUMMARY

(Erase heading not required.)

Army Form C. 2118

Hen HQ NCW Bases 17 Div   February 1916

Place	Date	Hour	Summary of Events and Information	Remarks and references to Appendices
Rouen	12	5 p.m.	Truck 5744, 4 ton general stores. Truck 18257, 167 cases of P.H. Helmets for 2nd Army to Dept. HQHW	
"	13	6 p.m.	Truck 73696, 5 ton general stores. Truck 9617 with 460 general stores, including 200 T.P. Helmets. HQHW	
"	14	5 p.m.	Truck 87136 containing 6 tons of general stores. HQHW	
"	15	6 p.m.	76 Inf Infy Brigade arrived for duty under Brim. Truck 17686 containing 2 tons general stores. Went to 3rd Division for Bert & Coy to report here for duty. Truck 76167 B.D.S. HQHW	
"	16	5 p.m.	Pte Edmondson Gun hook expert, reported here for duty. Truck 165372 containing 6 tons ground stores, including 100 Stew Helmets. HQHW Collects 30 Nr of Periscopes from 29th Div for use in Rouen, owing	
	17		to losses in recent 15 trench HQHW. Owing to recent severe cold weather stores principally trench & kit war cap outages. Details not available. Truck 70724, containing 5 ton of general stores including 150 Steel Helmets & Truck 57676, wrt 100 cases of Tout Helmets HQHW	

Army Form C. 2118

WAR DIARY
or
INTELLIGENCE SUMMARY
(Erase heading not required.)

Army Troops HQ ADSS
17 Division
February 1916

Place	Date	Hour	Summary of Events and Information	Remarks and references to Appendices
Remingheest	18th	8 p.c.	Lieut Colonel Holland & Major Statham took over of 3rd Div reports here for duty with 76 Bde. 40th Bde R.F.A. of 3rd Div arrived for attachment to this Divn. Truck 8885 containing 4 tons general stores. Truck 136031 containing 1 Caul W.D.6 Tank. H.P.D	
"	19	5 p.c.	Steam not running. Railway work often midday, making railway work take a more difficult. Truck 23004 containing 6 tons general stores including axe. Elect. Holmes. H.P.D	
"	20	70 k	Truck 23031 containing 7 tons general stores. Truck 17496 with 2 Civ Officers men. All personnel of 50th & 57th Bde are lost in recent action. Now replaced by return from Base. H.P.D	
"	21	40 k	Truck 57743 containing 4 tons general stores & 4 machine guns to replace ones in recent action. Storm still running lost at Railhead. H.P.D Truck 77804 containing 6 tons general stores. H.P.D	
"	22	830		
"	23	5 p.c.	Truck 161587 containing 4 tons general stores & Lewis Guns. Truck 160015 92 tanks & 4 Lewis Guns to France 29658. 39579 with which. Cant only unload. Truck 150515 at Railhead closed for dismantling. H.P.D	

Army Form C. 2118

WAR DIARY
or
INTELLIGENCE SUMMARY

(Erase heading not required.)

H.Q. Welsh Div
R.A.D.S. 17 D.A.C
January 1916

Instructions regarding War Diaries and Intelligence Summaries are contained in F. S. Regs., Part II. and the Staff Manual respectively. Title Pages will be prepared in manuscript.

Place	Date	Hour	Summary of Events and Information	Remarks and references to Appendices
Romarin	24	7 p	Truck #147754 containing 9 tons general stores HQ72	
"	25	6/sp	Lorry receives from 3rd Div for work over 76th Bde. Truck 88165 containing 9 tons incendiary machine gun for 7th Borders HQ72	
"	26	5 p	Truck 8076 containing 7 tons general stores HQ72	
"	27	6 p	Lieut K.S. Morgan arrives to assist work 3rd Div units now attached collects 1100 steel helmets from 1st & 2nd Canadian Div & 3060 for spares issues to 76th Bde. Truck 3883 containing 7 tons general stores Truck 15080 containing 4 tons clothing & T.P. Helmets Truck 8980 with 40 bales blankets HQ72	
"	28	5 p	Truck 147072 with 5 tons general stores HQ72	
"	29	9 p	Truck 20887 with 2 tons general stores HQ72	

HQ Welsh Front
29/1/16 RADDS 17 DAC

DUDOS
17DW
Vol 8

Army Form C. 2118

WAR DIARY
or
INTELLIGENCE SUMMARY

March 1916   H.Q. War Fd Depot 17 Div

(Erase heading not required.)

Instructions regarding War Diaries and Intelligence Summaries are contained in F.S. Regs., Part II. and the Staff Manual respectively. Title Pages will be prepared in manuscript.

Place	Date	Hour	Summary of Events and Information	Remarks and references to Appendices
Reninghelst	1	5p	Issued 120471 units 6 tons of general stores HT72	
"	2	6p	8th Lofty Bdes ammn for attachment to Divn. Cav was up to Wormhoudt Avenue with Zylone to draw for 76th Bde. Issued 3032 a 24843 units 12 tons of general stores HT72	
	3	5p	Issued 63827 units 9 tons genl stores HT45	
	4	6p	11114 6 tons genl stores HT72	
	5	7p	265732 10 tons general stores. HQn - 470 gun park through by lorry HQn	
	6	5p	40306 u 1386 from gun park through HT72	
	7	6p	Arranges to move to Steenvoorde on mob. to 2nd Corps HT72	
Steenvoorde	8	5p	Moves to Steenvoorde Hn	
"	9	6p	Routine work. Issued 57665 & 23338 units general stores HT72	
Mervin	10	7p	Issued 150767 units 10 tons general stores in charge Lieut Gun 1st 10th Notts Derby moves dump to Mervin HT72	

1875. Wt. W593/826 1,000,000 4/15 J.B.C. & A.   A.D.S.S./Forms/C. 2118.

WAR DIARY or INTELLIGENCE SUMMARY

Army Form C. 2118

Troops. 17 Division

March 1916

Place	Date	Hour	Summary of Events and Information	Remarks and references to Appendices
Meaulte	11	5 p.c.	Truck 95766 with 7 tons general stores, a lewis gun for 1st A	
"	12	9 p.c.	Yprès. also Truck 55727 with one wagon G.S. HQRS	
"	13	5 p.c.	Truck 2944 with 4 tons general stores & one lewis gun for 7th Lin. Regt HQRS	
"	14	9 p.c.	Truck 87327 with 3 tons general stores HQRS	
"	15	7 p.c.	Rations & work HQRS	
"	16	5 p.c.	Truck 4509 with 4 tons general stores HQRS	
"			Truck 42229 with 3 tons general stores & Truck 1058 with clothing HQRS	
"	17		Truck 161654 with 4 tons general stores HQRS	
"	18		Truck 24314 with 4 tons general stores, including lewis gun & 1500 Steel Helmets, also Truck 2948 with clothing HQRS	
"	19th	8 p.c.	Truck 130216 with 4 Tons general stores. Took over duties DADOS from Capt. T.J. Keller PSH	
"	20th to	8 p.c.	" 404-24 with 5 Tons General stores. Capt. T.J. Keller proceeded to England on leave PSH	
"	21st	9 p.c.	Moved to Pont de Nieppe. Truck 104462 with 4 Ton general stores. PSH	

WAR DIARY or INTELLIGENCE SUMMARY

(Erase heading not required.)

Army Form C. 2118

D.A.D.O.S. 17th Division.

March 1916.

Instructions regarding War Diaries and Intelligence Summaries are contained in F.S. Regs., Part II. and the Staff Manual respectively. Title Pages will be prepared in manuscript.

Place	Date	Hour	Summary of Events and Information	Remarks and references to Appendices
P. de Nieppe	22nd	8 a/c	Truck 99336 with 6 Tons general stores. RKhr	
"	23rd	7 a/c	Truck 3809 with 4 Tons general stores. RKhr	
"	24th	8 a/c	Truck 62922 with 7 Tons general stores and 300 French Helmets RKhr	
"	25th	8 a/c	Truck 152143 with 4 Tons general stores RKhr	
"	26th	8 a/c	Truck 56335 with 5 Tons general stores and 1500 French Helmets RKhr	
"	27th	—	Truck 23786 with general stores and 500 French Helmets RKhr	
"	27th	9 a/c	Truck 22603 with 2 Tons general stores RKhr	
"	—	—	Truck 196 with 1 wagon limbered R.E. complete for 17th Div. Sig. Coy. R.E. RKhr	
"	28th	9 a/c	Truck 160494 with 1 Ton general stores and 1 Lewis gun for 9th North'n Fus. RKhr	
"	29th	8 a/c	Truck 130003 with 4 Tons general stores RKhr	
"	30th	8 a/c	Truck 151616 with 6 Tons general stores RKhr	
"	31st	8 a/c	Truck 40424 with 7 Tons general stores and 2 stone fonts for withdrawal of winter clothing. 1 N.C.O. and 12 men 51st F.A. reported 9 a.m. for duty re winter clothing. RKhr	

31/3/16.

R Murray Lieut:
D.O.O. 17th Div:

D.A.G.
3rd Echelon
Base.

Herewith a copy of Lieut. R.S. Murray's diary, who was acting DADOS during April last.
The original was sent to you, but I understand from my D.H.Q. that it is not to hand.

H.J. Weller Capt.
DADOS 17th Div.

31/2/6

Army Form C. 2118

DADOS 17th Division
April 1916. Vol 9

WAR DIARY
or
INTELLIGENCE SUMMARY
(Erase heading not required.)

Instructions regarding War Diaries and Intelligence Summaries are contained in F. S. Regs., Part II. and the Staff Manual respectively. Title Pages will be prepared in manuscript.

Place	Date	Hour	Summary of Events and Information	Remarks and references to Appendices
Pontoillepp	1st	8²/c	Truck 40192 with 6 tons General Stores including 13 wheels, wantsoats (gys) R.S.M.	
			Gys of Jerkins Leather taken in from units	
"	2nd	9²/c	Truck 148712 with 7 tons Gonsolidatones (gys) R.S.M.	
"	3rd	9²/c	Truck 58607 with 1 ton General stones. (gys) R.S.M.	
"	4th	8²/c	Truck 85041 with 2 tons General stones (gys) R.S.M.	
"	5th	8²/c	Truck 23381 with 5 tons General stones (gys) R.S.M.	
"	6th	8²/c	Truck 57630 with 5 tons General stones (gys) R.S.M.	
"	7th	8²/c	Truck 29582 with 6 tons General stones (gys) R.S.M.	
"	8th	8²/c	Truck 57268 with 8 tons General stones (gys) R.S.M.	
"	9th	8²/c	Truck 60677 with 5 tons General stones	
			Truck 4881 with 1 Waggon S for R.I. By Division (gys) R.S.M.	
"	10th	8²/c	Truck 70107 with 3 tons General stones. (gys) R.S.M.	
"	11th	8²/c	Truck 161225 with 1 ton General stones (gys) R.S.M.	
"	12th	8²/c	Truck 29901 with 4 tons General stones	
			Truck 1828 with 2 carts watertank for D/81 Ya Bde & 7th yn L By Boy R.S.M	
"	13th	8²/c	Truck 24487 with 6 tons General stones	
			Truck 135788 with 2 bodies & 2 Limber Kitch travelling for 12th Frankelson(?) (w) R.S.M	
"	14th	8²/c	Truck 87093 with 8 tons General stones (gys) R.S.M.	
"	15th	8²/c	Truck 159012 with 6 tons General stones including 29 cases "D.H" Helmets, also Truck 161093 with 250 cases "P.H" Helmets (gys) R.S.M	

Army Form C. 2118

WAR DIARY
or
INTELLIGENCE SUMMARY
(Erase heading not required.)

Copy

D.A.D.O.S. 17th Division
April 1916

Place	Date	Hour	Summary of Events and Information	Remarks and references to Appendices
P. de Neppe	16th	9 p/c	Truck 42487 with 5 tons general stores (ags) R.S.R.	
"	17th	9 p/c	Truck 22869 with 3 tons general stores (ags) R.S.R.	
"	18th	9 p/c	Truck 42487 with 1 ton general stores (ags) R.S.R.	
"	19th	9 p/c	Truck 83678 with 3 tons general stores (ags) R.S.R.	
"			Truck 54579 with 2 Kitchens travelling, Bodies for 9th North'd Fus: and 1 Scots Gds. (ags) R.S.R.	
"	20th	8 p/c	Truck 846.18 with for 1st West Riding Regt. 4 tons general stores (ags) R.S.R.	
"	21st	8 p/c	Truck 130538 with 6 tons general stores (ags) R.S.R.	
"	22nd	8 p/c	Truck 55238 with 3 tons general stores, including 1 Bicycle + 1 Gun Limber for 8th So. Staff: (ags) R.S.R.	
"	23rd	8 p/c	Truck 6002 with 5 tons general stores (3yd) R.S.R.	
"	24th	8 p/c	Truck 138070 with 1 ton general stores. Includes 250 Trench Helmets (ags) R.S.R.	
"	25th	8 p/c	Truck 165422 with 4 tons general stores.	
"			Truck 41 with 1 Cart Water Tank for 6th Dorsets (ags) R.S.R.	
"	26th	8 p/c	Truck 8954 with 5 tons general stores (ags) R.S.R.	
"	27th	8 p/c	Truck 52265 with 5 tons general stores.	
"			Truck 2349 with 2 Limbers Kitchen travelling for (2nd North'd Fus.-7gns) R.S.R.	
"	28th	8 p/c	Truck 131868 with 3 tons general stores, including 1 Lewis Gun for 10th war form. (ags) R.S.R.	
"	29th	8 p/c	Truck 4914 with 5 tons general stores (ags) R.S.R.	
"	30th	8 p/c	Truck 908 with 3 tons general stores	
"			Truck 16907 with 1 - 4.5" Howr Carriage without fittings for 73/81st Howr Bdy.	

Left base on 29th inst.

(ags) R.S.R. Murray Lt.
DDD 17th Dn'y

Certified true copy
H Stewart Capt
DADOS 17th Div
3/5/16

1875. Wt. W503/826 1,000,000 4/15 J.B.C. & A. A.D.S.S./Forms/C. 2118/16

WAR DIARY or INTELLIGENCE SUMMARY

Army Form C. 2118

7th Division

May 1916

(Erase heading not required.)

Place	Date	Hour	Summary of Events and Information	Remarks and references to Appendices
P. da Niego	1/5/16	8 a/c	Truck 36730 with 3 Tons general stores. RSh	
"	2/5/16	8 a/c	Truck 61054 with 2 Tons general stores. RSh	
"	3/5/16	8 a/c	Truck 1452 with 4 Tons general stores including 1000 Sand Sandbags. RSh	
"	4/5/16	8 a/c	Truck 139490 with 4 Tons Stores	
"			Truck 6438 with 5½ gun team complete. RSh	
"	5/5/16	8 a/c	Truck 7163 with 9 Tons general stores including 24 Wheels. RSh	
"	6/5/16	8 a/c	Truck 168415 with 35 Tons general stores RSh	
"			Truck 7683 with 1 Conf W.T. for 7 Border Regt. RSh	
"	7/5/16	8 a/c	Truck 12438 with 4 Tons general stores. RSh	
"	8/5/16	8 a/c	Truck 40635 with 4 Tons general stores RSh	
"	9/5/16	8 a/c	Truck 9273 with 4 Tons general stores. RSh	
"	10/5/16	8 a/c	Truck 167204 with 3 Tons general stores. Ruin Board complete for H.Q. 20th Infantry Bde. 7/C. Conf W.T. for 12 Punch.	
"			Truck 14134 with 1 Wagon Ruin Board complete for H.Q. 20th Infantry Bde. 7/C. Conf W.T. for 12 Punch. RSh	
"	11/5/16	8 a/c	Truck 1023 with 5 Van general stores RSh	
"	12/4/16	7 a/c	" 4524 " 6 tons general stores RSh	
"	13/4/16	7 a/c	No truck owing to uppearing move of Divn. RSh	
"	14/4/16	8 a/c	Routine work, picking stores in dump for removal RSh	
Tilgue	15/5	7 a/c	Moved Dump of Offices to Tilgue. RSh	
"	16/5	8/4	Divn Sup Dump of Offices & Tilgue open. Tour 3556 with 1 Ton rations ex stores. Rations Stamps egn 6 RSh	

WAR DIARY or INTELLIGENCE SUMMARY

Army Form C. 2118

2nd Stage

May 1916

(Erase heading not required.)

Place	Date	Hour	Summary of Events and Information	Remarks and references to Appendices
Tdepin	17	8 a.m.	Truck 13982 with 5 tons gend stores ATyrs.	
"	18	7 p.c.	" 15240 " 4 tons of gend clothes ATyrs	
"	19	1 p.c.	Railhead Walten. Truck 82061 ½ truck 4 tons gend stores 2 lorries zone & Calais for 10000 shorts & spare boots to be rail'd direct to Rest Area	ATyrs
	20	7 p.	Truck with 7 tons of gend stores	ATyrs
	21	8 p.	Truck 164590 with 3 tons gend clothes	ATyrs
	22	7 p.c.	Truck 1237 with 2 tons gend clothes stores, a lot of tarpaulin lent ??? returned from camps & fill up for II Corps Troops, and 5703 2am rail Tnr 1307.	ATyrs
	23	77.	Truck 152142 with 1 lot gend clothes, 2 trucks 5 97.6 with 2000 Helmets T-P. Sow artillery stores to troop @ Trinture. 1070	ATyrs
	24		Truck 42844 with 3 tons 7 gend clothes, a tarra 2832 with 52 wheels	ATyrs

WAR DIARY or INTELLIGENCE SUMMARY

Army Form C. 2118

VCS/10

STAFF 17 Division 3rd Echelon

May 1916

Place	Date	Hour	Summary of Events and Information	Remarks and references to Appendices
Tilguar	25	9 p	Truck 22930 north 7 ton of gen. stores aleo truck 53923 north one wag. G.S.	
"	26	7 p	Truck 86676 north 7 ton gen. stores, went to Pountainh to obtain Stokes Ammunition Carriers, o equipment for carrying Lewis magazines TTBW	
"	27	8 p	Truck 493 with 11 ton gen. stores including 25 Verdeck cases	
"	28	7 p	1 truck 89177 north 6 ton of gen. stores. Second Army Artillery School at Tilgner to be supplied by us. whilst at Tilgner. 2nd Ammunition TM 1417, 27 R TTBW	
"	29	8 p	Truck 22449 north 6 ton of general stores. Truck TTBW 4924 north 2499 T Steel Helmets TTBW	
"	30	7 p	Truck 6320 north 3 ton of general stores TTBW	
"	31	8 p	Truck 40323 north 6 ton of general stores TTBW	

H.T. Weller Capt.
D.A.D.O.S. 17 Div
31/5/16

WAR DIARY or INTELLIGENCE SUMMARY

Army Form C. 2118

D.A.D.O.S. 17 Division / 1st Staff

June 1916

Place	Date	Hour	Summary of Events and Information	Remarks and references to Appendices
Talgras	1st	8p	Tmvek 21776 went 8 box of gnd stores	ATM
"	2nd	7pc	Tmvek 497 took 6 box of gnd stores & Tmvek 15 & stores & other	ATM
"	3	6p	Tmvek 1264 went 5 box gnd stores	ATM
"	4	7pc	Tmvek 61410 went 6 box 1 gnd stores	ATM
"	5	7pc	Tmvek 62538 went 3 box of gnd stores & Tmvek 58252 went 15 cwt load for trench mortar. Pte J.H. Todge at command of tmvek 7103 for man. o. 7pm rec 19/1916 – Regtl. or tmvek 2nd K LR 1916	ATM
"	6	5pc	Tmvek 98325 went 1 box of gnd stores	ATM
"	7	7pc	Tmvek 41075 went 4 box of gnd stores	ATM
"	8	10pc	Tmvek 988 went 6 box of gnd stores	ATM
"	9	2.30	Tmvek no tmver preparing to move 17 4 L army area	ATM
Hilly	10	9pc	No tmvek. Routine work	ATM
Allonville	11	0	No tmvek. Left for train to connect XV Corp w per DAQ Secret move m Allonville	ATM

1875 Wt. W593/826 1,000,000 4/15 J.B.C. & A. A.D.S.S./Forms/C. 2118.

WAR DIARY or INTELLIGENCE SUMMARY

Army Form C. 2118

Pages 1780
Vol II
June 1916

Place	Date	Hour	Summary of Events and Information	Remarks and references to Appendices
Allonville	12th	8p	Store tent came by Rail from Tidworth. Brought SS Cart & WC Army	MPW
"	13	9a	Arrived. Routine work & unrigging Ramps &c	MPW
"	14	6p	Truck 6473 from Mont Buch just	MPW
"	15	9a	Routine work. No truck. Removed & Damp new N4 Bringing train	MPW
"	16	9a	Routine work. No truck	MPW
"	17	8p	Truck 64079. Clothing	MPW
"	18	7a	Truck 148314. Routine work	MPW
"	19	6p	Truck No 41417 & 7475 with Bath grenades & uniform & gun store	MPW
"	20	7p	No truck. Routine work	MPW
"	21	8p	Truck 97814, 5360, & 132045 with Clothing. Truck Helmer & Boots respectively	MPW
"	22	7p	also Truck 531 with vehicles	MPW
"	23	6p	Truck 7474 Lewis magazines & Oil & fuzes	MPW
"	24	9a	Truck 16732 Wheel, Gas goggles, Knocker gun & SOL $207	MPW
"	25	6p	Truck 64069 with clothing	MPW
"	26	9p	Truck 21034 lying Shot. Truck 25285 Clothing	MPW

Army Form C. 2118

WAR DIARY
or
INTELLIGENCE SUMMARY

Dvsn. 17 Bn 3rd Sec[tion]

June 1916

(Erase heading not required.)

Instructions regarding War Diaries and Intelligence Summaries are contained in F.S. Regs., Part II. and the Staff Manual respectively. Title Pages will be prepared in manuscript.

Place	Date	Hour	Summary of Events and Information	Remarks and references to Appendices
Allouarde minioni-	27th	8 p/m	Trench 5799. Tube Helmets & Sprayers	from
L.APR	28	7 p/m	Moved Dump to movement. Trench 16539 with Rails.	APW
			2 Trench 13145 with 25 Gas Cyln Land Cart	APW
			Gun for Rep[air] & Pick up Lorry from Altevans	APW
	29	8 p/m	Trench 2436	APW
	30	6 p/m	Trench 26943. Keeper chan.	APW

H.T. Weller Capt
Dvsn. 17 Bn

30/6/16

WAR DIARY or INTELLIGENCE SUMMARY

Army Form C. 2118

1st S.A.I. — D.A.P.O.S. — 9th July — 9th Division — Vol 12 — July 1916

Place	Date	Hour	Summary of Events and Information	Remarks and references to Appendices
Morcourt – 1st July to 4th	1st	8 p.c.	Truck 4664 with butter oil, & 19 lamb stew truck, also Truck 5756 with apparatus running out (8 bundles) & 29 Lewis hammocks. Very fairly well day, a good report received on & forward hammocks. DTH @ at Truck	DTH
"	2nd	8 p.c.	Truck 152899 with Pat Respirators & gas alarms. DTH removed to Ribemont. All spare running out sent by Bass & Cooper Workshops & Base orderly cancelled. Then started frontline delivery.	DTH
"	3rd	8 p.	Truck 153364 gas goggles & clothing. Owing to the continuous rain damage coming to jersey for 70 & 29 parks. A spring running out. Bare serviced to keep a constant reserve as to requirements. Heavy firing all day & many German prisoners in Company. Heavy lost arrange for Lewis & machine guns to be sent from Allerville. The same must have an own 18 Pdr. Ser. moved to for all 9.30 p.m. a convoy by lorry at Railhead at 10.30 p.m.	DTH
"	4th		Truck 145128 with Respirators & Sponges for DTH and 2" mortar & spare parts taken forward for issue & application to 62 Army Workshops at Beauval. Truck times were then 8.9 a.m.	DTH

WAR DIARY or INTELLIGENCE SUMMARY

Army Form C. 2118

D.A.D.O.S. 17 Division 2nd Sheet July 1916

Place	Date	Hour	Summary of Events and Information	Remarks and references to Appendices
Thiennes la Attre	5th	a.p.	Truck 137029 Brick boat, gd stores & 160 Stretchers. DHQ. a killed severe HQ on Bayout to Meaulte Road. 2250 Fwd Dressings sent to Stretcher by Special Lorry Convoy. Held up for 2 hours by heavy shell fire. Between Meaulte - Fricourt. Heavy demand for Dressings Bandages, etc. & Machine Gun & implants received from DHQ that wound Ord now supplied in two that affect ship a arrow of 10 per opening. Referred to C.R.A. for further report. 7 HH	
	6th		Truck 63615 bulk anti-freezing oil & grease & 1932 and 250 Stretchers & water bottles. 52,466 units vehicles. DHQ service including for work battle that equipped. But Park will ship all off all under clothes & boots any change ware men's clothing in relay. Supervision Lieut Pearse HHG tour two collects per Lounge to equip Park	
	7		Truck 167484 bulk Stretchers, a Box Respirators & 4758 units vehicles. motor gaunt run to Army workshop for R/R. necessarian for 2. T. motorlan 30 T.M. Handcart for Bdr @ Becourd. DHQ cannot accept for present Been report that tired T.M.C odd. not up to Stand and for work regard. Auto & wheel not strong enough, & woodwork badly finished HHG	

WAR DIARY or INTELLIGENCE SUMMARY

3rd Sheet. R.A.D.O.S. 17th Divis Army Form C. 2118

July 1916

Place	Date	Hour	Summary of Events and Information	Remarks and references to Appendices
Meriaucourt La Alp	8th		Truck 139257 with clothing, a 12 Pennant Sprayers, a 18 par aircon flares for O/C Rev., also Truck 71° 9 with vehicles. BTHp received all Tiraphra to be sent to this Office, for transmission to Base. Instruct. to arrange on Sat. on parade 57th Rev who have lost wait equipment in frame regiment. TJW	
"	9		Truck 41084 with clothing & gent stores. 3590 complete arts for infantry and Rev also 2468 sets Taken to 7th Brigadl Armn to be issued with to Cavillon to arrange for Dump. TJW	
Cavillon	10		Truck 27667 with clothing 2400 Shirts a 3000 S.D. Trousers with care of portion of Artillery men's haul & davison for tea a re equipping RHHP at Cavillon. Railhead at Heign depot. Now in 2nd Corps area. TJW	
"	11		Truck 42183 with tins clothing etc. completing RE equipment. TJW	
"	12		Truck 280229 with boots & gent stores. Rodens work. TJW	
"	13		Rodens work. Sent truck a cased rifles for Artillery Truck 33585 Parth Out & wheels. Truck 600 mult needs 2 Brs TJW	

WAR DIARY
or
INTELLIGENCE SUMMARY

Army Form C. 2118

D.A.D.O.S. 17 bis
4th Army
July 1916

Place	Date	Hour	Summary of Events and Information	Remarks and references to Appendices
Tt Euveille	6th/14	7¾	Tanks 153228 held - Issue cases, Trucks 153228 and 188900 at Yukon gun now returned from Allonville as 11th Div. are not now Ration-ed to day. The gun/r 57/8 despatched by Army to I.O.M. XX Corps, with detail about for Ambitious, now accumulating by 21 Div. 57/8	
Pont-Remy/15 Somme		7¾	No truck. Troops went today to new position. Good dump at 2 o'clock this square. Warehouse Canny & 3rd section of Smiths Rationed a Foggles. Lorries had to make 3 journeys. Here notes that Reserve Trench to dumped	
"	16	7¾	Trucks 2 to 137 including 11 hundred of Gunnup running out for BTFC These transferred by road to 21st Div. by whom BTFC are being eliminated. Returned to Allonville one vickers gun 15203 in & on, also machine armament. Have informed DHQ of the matter, in view of its importance of conserving all machine guns & parts during present operation.	BTf

Army Form C. 2118

5th Sect'n DADOS 17 Division

WAR DIARY
or
INTELLIGENCE SUMMARY

(Erase heading not required.)

July 1916

Place	Date	Hour	Summary of Events and Information	Remarks and references to Appendices
Pont Remy (Somme)	17th	7p.	No truck today, having been cancelled owing to Div'l movements. Went to Lierco on probable way to let a Bn Respirators for Machine Gunners owing to shortage of equipment already carried. Before returning to Corps have asked DADOS for instruction. It appears many Box Respirators are issued as general issue action, whereas in [fact?] by numbers [exchange?] Since July 1st. Sect'n of Special Action 36 members have been demanded by Corps on — Respirator etc —	HQ
"	18	7p.	No truck. Routine work.	HQ
"	19	7p.	Truck 26850. Bulk clothing, boots etc. Railhead Longpré. Have urgent on to IX Corps as exchange, but now fewer gloves. HQ	
"	20		Truck 19709. Bulk out on Scope 21, a 29102 met [?] war ammt [?] same car of 50RR 7 to G Coy underms on MTs trying to carry on [?] HQ	

WAR DIARY or INTELLIGENCE SUMMARY

Army Form C. 2118

6th Sheet   DAYS 17 to
                   July 1916

(Erase heading not required.)

Place	Date	Hour	Summary of Events and Information	Remarks and references to Appendices
Pont Remy Somme	21	7 p.c.	Urgent wire for 5152d Hermite store is Bme, to replace it, impressment 2020 diary ampules in Tmunk 180098 was bulk horse-sprayer	HJN
"	22	7 p.c.	Tmunk 21065 bulk clothing & sprayers. Have procured material for Regt. hedge set Bgh BORS' knege and howeer bos indicate to obtain locally, so must do w/o on private industries	HJN
Ribémont	23	7 p.c.	Wires for rearm to XVI Corps, and received at Albert but no news on K Relieving Arm cannot arrange in consequence to transfer 1 Anti Smoke Helmet. Tmunk 35953 wires cycles & Lewis Handcart also 227032 B and 31 Lewis Hand Carts. Moved Bump to "Ribémont" now north 15th Corps	HJN
"	24	7 p.c.	Tmunk 35955 with rifle 68031 with Respirators clothing 2 16 Lewis Hand Carts & 3524 with 15 Lewis Hand Carts. Wire from Ribémont Station Subarge Bump 12 Lewis Arm Carts & grenades 1 Bomb commun. magazine cannon & other useful stores for immediate issue	HJN

WAR DIARY
or
INTELLIGENCE SUMMARY

(Erase heading not required.)

7th Sqn STAFF 17th July 1916

Army Form C. 2118

Place	Date	Hour	Summary of Events and Information	Remarks and references to Appendices
Rikamont	25	7p	To trucks 16 day. Have Gas & Ammonia or repairing Salvaged SPAA Helmets, and contents for Brune for spare hoses. A match for same.	
"	26		7 mulls 200033 will both leave magazine & 8283 will contain contents from Brune. Not arrived at Meaulen or Albert also no trace of Gun & Carrige used by Order 9th Corps 9.C.61 of 23/7/16	
"	27		Turner 15%0241 treated army refum, one a spares. Arrived to Bout Remy to see if Reserve of 13000 Small Helmets kept for 14th Div has been taken over. Has refum over 21th Div aut. Q x). of 25/7/16, in answer to letter that 3rd Army had arranged for 14th Div to take over the Reserve notes of 21th Div. The Helmets not yet taken over. Have referred matter to DV Corps for instructions.	

WAR DIARY or INTELLIGENCE SUMMARY

Army Form C. 2118

D.A.D.O.S. 17 Div

July 1916

Place	Date	Hour	Summary of Events and Information	Remarks and references to Appendices
Lesboeufs	28	7 p.c	No trucks from Acheux. Trucks 46280 until 53102 unloaded from morning, also morning (?) 50 m.g. Coy, from Albrincis Trench 2204 with 5 Vickers Guns. Trucks 20507S unloaded Lewis Magazine ammt at Acheux this day late, also Trucks 84487 at? ammunition. Trucks 53106 early for S.A.A. m.g. Coy in SOS m.g. Coy. SAA early late also. Horse ammt 21 tons for parties of ammunition S.A.A. mortar Ricos (?) they report at our trench ... at our H.Q. F.T.M ??	
"	29	7 p.c	Truck 21027) SAA. but no ammunition. Truck 49242 SAA. but has not arrived.	
"	30	7 p.c	Trucks 49242 SAA. but has not arrived. Have reports of large a.a.m.p. the decay experienced at Albert. A consigneurs stoppage of ammunition seen	
"	31	7 p.c	Trucks 21027) has been when a clothing due on 27th amounts to any. " 49242 " general stores " 30 " " " 1365 due to Hay manure SAA. Parcels etc. not yet to hand. " 573 OS until repair the Acheux ammo movement. Demand for most to Acheux to late now from 5 Div Division TFM	

Army Form C. 2118

WAR DIARY
or
INTELLIGENCE SUMMARY

(Erase heading not required.)

July 1916

Place	Date	Hour	Summary of Events and Information	Remarks and references to Appendices
Beaumont Hamel	31		Continued. Generally speaking during the period in question the month, supplies have come up with a promptly from the Base, especially all returns of S.A.A., Trench mortars & machine guns, the system of drawing an advance depot at Acheux, a the system of sending by intermediate train a Limber teams as needed invariably to quick supply of these important stores. The principal shortages have been Steel Helmets, Leon Magazine Lewis Gun Haversacks, & [illeg] to a lesser degree wire cutters S.A. No 1. There have all been accumulated in the base through Ordnance. A good deal has been recovered through Salvage, though not appreciated Mule up ad horses 36 mules from been obtained as reserves [signature] Base during the month. [signature]	

Army Form C. 2118

Vol 13

1st Sk. Rif. D.A.D.O.S. 17 / 17 Div

WAR DIARY or INTELLIGENCE SUMMARY
(Erase heading not required.)

August 1916

Place	Date	Hour	Summary of Events and Information	Remarks and references to Appendices
Rainmont	1	7 p	To truck received at Albert last reports waiting to TP & Corps	
E.10.B. O.C.I.P		7 p.c	Preparing to remove dump to new area ETA	
"	2	7 p.c	Removed dump to a Field Depot. E.10.B. new Albert laterly occupied by 51st Div. Truck 1365 Amm Shed & late Heavies a 20578 grub stores & horses. Truck 53358 inst vehicle & Harness Hart letter way 5th Div. R.a. 13th F.amb & 5th Mot Ven. ETA	
"	3	7 p.c	Truck 21036B truck took Held up on Railroad for 4 hours owing to enemy shelling	7p.c
"	4	7 p.c	Received now moves to Fricly Truck	7p.c
"	5	7 p.c	Truck 15/63 Bulk clothing & bundle running but opening for DAC	
"	6	7 p.c	Truck 20833C (22 Div.) inst. 5 bundles running missing ETA	

WAR DIARY
or
INTELLIGENCE SUMMARY

(Erase heading not required.)

Army Form C. 2118

2nd Sec. STABS 17 Division August 1916

Instructions regarding War Diaries and Intelligence Summaries are contained in F.S. Regs., Part II. and the Staff Manual respectively. Title Pages will be prepared in manuscript.

Place	Date	Hour	Summary of Events and Information	Remarks and references to Appendices
Trias Paper E.10.B T. Allen near Allen	7	7⁷/c	Moved camp away from previous position on account of shell fire, & also owing to proximity to Hozan line, & much traffic. Tower 15717 enclosing 5.0 cylrs. & dry respirators. Iron magazine, also Tower 71575 with 1 span comprising 3 R.O. Sid eight for c/78 Beer Rtja	
"	8	7⁷/c	Instructs the eyster of no. 6. doing anti or ordinary Gypsies. Tower 24424 with 18pan Shields & 2 sorts of power frame. & general stores.	
"	9	7⁷/c	Tower 64872 with bull leads, & numing new opening to STPC, also	
"	10	7⁷/c	Tower 26477 enclosing 14 R.O Springs, & accum acc R.O Springs now vacated are to be moved to I O M	

WAR DIARY or INTELLIGENCE SUMMARY

Army Form C. 2118

3rd Sheet — 17 Divn — August 1916

Place	Date	Hour	Summary of Events and Information	Remarks and references to Appendices
Near Albert	11	7 p.c.	Petrol Dump at Albert now completely destroyed by enemy's fire. All stores were however removed before this took place. Trucks 1192 north Ro Spring (loads now to IOM 15 tons). 137157. Empties have gone to where 90750. — Manilla	HW
	12	7 p.c.	No news of anything exc[ept] impending move. Last received all [cars] from Rnes except for 5 Divn Units now under a supervates clerk and no known a vehicle park.	
Albert	13	7 p.c.	Moved Dump to Rebommer. Transferred 5th Divn units to 14th Divn Trunk Jan 12 not removing motor lorries from Granges.	
	14	7 p.c.	Transferred 17th Supply Col to 17 Arm. Sup Park to 10 Corps on their arr. Leaving this train. No news from Hunts. Issued Army accts or Ltg coke cheese — administered by Baloa from 15th — manual ext[...]	

Army Form C. 2118

4th ACS gos. WAR DIARY STABLES. 17 Pw
or
INTELLIGENCE SUMMARY   August 1916
(Erase heading not required.)

Instructions regarding War Diaries and Intelligence
Summaries are contained in F. S. Regs., Part II.
and the Staff Manual respectively. Title Pages
will be prepared in manuscript.

Place	Date	Hour	Summary of Events and Information	Remarks and references to Appendices
Rubempré	15	7.0c	Preparing to meet Dump & Place over in truck	HQw
Bavelincourt	16	7.0c	No truck. Office in ?HQ? Dump moved on to Henu	HQw
Henu	17	7.0c	No truck. Office in Bowlum with ?HQ? purchased items & arranged to carry over Dump from 56 Div. Also arranged to obtain 2T Pirt receipt of Empire Helmets with 52 Div. There in Reserve. Went to collect to 56 Div Railhead	HQw
"	18	7.0c	Routine work	HQw
"	19	7.0c	Truck 76505 with 128 Rounds of Hotchkiss Sets have been dumped on to Dump	HQw
"	20	7.0c	Truck 24 611 with 8 Tons grd cloth a 18 pm for 9/78 Regt. Have arranged to take over 7gun Ammunition. Position as at Tanks Shops	HQw
Henu	21	7.0c	Took Office & both over 62 tons Dumps. Truck 17337 with 8 tons grd cloth. Busy to cleaning Rudders without more. Sandly in 12 midnight or thrown much ?? & ho rupture on all concerned, as must avoid journeys the day & night.	HQw

Army Form C. 2118

WAR DIARY or INTELLIGENCE SUMMARY

(Erase heading not required.)

517 Sh:Cf- D.A.D.O.S. 17 Div.

August 1916

Place	Date	Hour	Summary of Events and Information	Remarks and references to Appendices
Ham	22	7 p.c.	Truck 182 with gun stores, 9619 with ℒ/bn clothing, 15267 with S.L. wheels & wagon parts. Many busy receipt owing to no stores being received for the past week. Conference with Baker Staff Captain re D.A.D. points & general riddance — such as workshops.	
"	23	7 p.c.	Truck 17309 with ℒ cltr gun stores & little be returned to Havre in ret'n Coy next day.	
"	24	7 p.c.	Rail Ammunition Coys moved stores. Had conference re Gnty 187 here — annexed to 14th army Cavalry	
"	25	7 p.c.	Truck 17540 with 1 lot of gun stores Raided	
"	26	12 p.c.	Proceeded on leave to England.	

H.W. Staller Capt.
A/D.A.D.O.S. 17 Div.

26/8/16

CONFIDENTIAL

WAR DIARY

OF

DADOS 17th DIVn

for

SEPT. 1916.

WAR DIARY or INTELLIGENCE SUMMARY

Army Form C. 2118.

10th yeat 17 A.T.S. 17 Division Sept 1916

Place	Date	Hour	Summary of Events and Information	Remarks and references to Appendices
Havre	3rd	10½	Returned from leave to England. HJW	HJW
"	4	19	Tannek 15829 wrote han 2nd class of 760 T.P Krennet HJW	
"	5	7½	Tannek 22054 " 2 brs " 404 "	HJW
"	"	7½	Tannek 91372 " 1 br " 3 Tannek 1603/hob yder HJW	
"	6	10½	Tannek 30246 " 1 br " 1 " 300 T.P Hecmck HJW	
"	7	7½	Tannek 47493 " 8 brs	HJW
"	8	7½	Tannek 99351 " 6 brs " 1 O 1 Dtwksch	HJW
"	9	7½	Tannek 65529 " 7 brs gave class of 300 T.R Helmets	HJW
"	10	7½	Tannek 41870 " 8 brs gave stores	HJW
"	11	7½	Tannek 139362 " 4 brs gave stores	HJW
"	12	7½	Tannek 210316 " 2 brs gave stores a Tannek 9016 mutt clarks	HJW
"	13	7½	Tannek 72759 " 4 brs of gave stores	HJW
"	14	7½	Tannek 57152 met 7 brs gave canvas a saddle for Supal	HJW
"	15	7½	Tannek 66555 met 10 brs gave stores	HJW
"	16	7½	Tannek 60465 " 6 brs gave costr unchroning 450 T.P Krenne	HJW
"	17	7½	Tannek 16189 wrote cross gave costr	HJW
"	18	7½	Tannek 3734 mett kloque	HJW
"	19	7½	Tannek 12670 mett Scott Supal	HJW

Instructions regarding War Diaries and Intelligence Summaries are contained in F.S. Regs., Part II. and the Staff Manual respectively. Title Pages will be prepared in manuscript.

Army Form C. 2118.

WAR DIARY
or
INTELLIGENCE SUMMARY
(Erase heading not required.)

2nd Sheet. STAFF, 17 2nd Army

Sept 1916

Place	Date	Hour	Summary of Events and Information	Remarks and references to Appendices
Hem	20	7¾	Carcass store from Bray, on instruction of move to Rail Area	
"	21		Routine work. Clearing up store from camp. Hrs arranged to hand over camp & salvage to incoming Divn.	
St Riquier	22	7.9	Remove to St Riquier	RJW
"	23	7.9.	Railhead St Riquier. Three trucks of coath which had been over in Regulating Station Abbeville when Divn was moving	RJW
"	24	7.9.	No stores received from Base. Routine work	
"	25	7.9.	No stores up to army. Routine work, inspecting Sanitation Stores.	RJW
"	26	7.6	10 ammn trucks arriving 4 Ap. to Regnier Bridge	RJW
"	27	7.10	Trucks 4403, 29580, 4403, 95751 unit clothing, Romilotys out slept hermit & good store	RJW
"	28	7.7	Truck 25880, 6577 units gen'l stores	RJW
"	29	7.30	Truck 34847 units 2 ton gen'l store	RJW
"	30	7.6	Truck 35277 ordnance Amn? 4ch to land. Routine work	RJW

30/9/16 H.Gresson Capt DSSO, 17 Divn

Confidential

Vol /5

WAR DIARY
of
DADOS 17th DIVISION

October, 1916.

Army Form C. 2118

WAR DIARY
or
INTELLIGENCE SUMMARY

(Erase heading not required.)

1st Sqdn SAADS 17 Division

October 1916

Place	Date	Hour	Summary of Events and Information	Remarks and references to Appendices
St Riquier	1	7	Tournai 5379 sent 7 km genl stores	RTN
"	2	7	Tournai 1223, 3 btn genl stores & 1 tram tpt to E. St Clept	RTN
"	3	7	& one 4.5 How for D/79 RFA	RTN
"	3	7	Tournai 56573 sent 160 genl stores a team from 76, for an addition 2 fce Balln. Owing to improving motor van cable stores from Poper. Sent Arty stores to PAS	
"	4	7	Had no truck today unable to recommence teams. Stores for 37th Sqdn RAC ones to Hedery & Saxilby RFA	
"	5	"	The Expn. Radios mtrd	RTN
PAS	6	"	Had no more Lamp, Stores to PAS, owing to under training meant at bottle 11 lorries taken to chut stores, shops & Reinmist Smura Hrmde	RTN
"	7	"	Tournai 47710 sent 13 ton 7 genl stores	RTN
"	8	"	No busses canvate owing to heavy traffic	RTN

WAR DIARY or INTELLIGENCE SUMMARY

Army Form C. 2118

2nd Sheet

Afghanistan [?] 17 Div

Oct. 1916

Place	Date	Hour	Summary of Events and Information	Remarks and references to Appendices
PAS	9	7¾	Transfer 4/870 & 5/8703 16 Kahars, work has been carried out	MTM
"	10	7⁰	Transfer 6/8215 want a how gun crew, have made a protest	MTM
"	11	7⁰	13 Transfer to relieve Havards on garrison	MTM
"	11	7⁹	Transfer 5/8904 want 1 hr gun store	MTM
"	12	7	Transfer 6739.9 want 7 hrs gun store, & M.G. Kutcha [?]/5522	MTM
"	13	7³⁰	Transfer 147218 want 3 hrs gun store	MTM
"	14	7	Transfer 6954 want 2 hrs gun store	M.9.9 6782
"	15	7¾	Transfer 140164 want 2 hrs gun store & 1 Lewis Gun to S.S Staff	MTM
"	16	-	Transfer 6777 want to have 9 hrs gun store & 2 Vicker gun	MTM
"	17	-	Transfer 32149 want 1 hr gun store & kitchen heads for 7 Brian Rgt.	MTM
"	18	-	Transfer 89152 want 2 hrs gun store	MTM
"	19	-	Transfer 37555 want 5 hrs gun store & 19172 4044 ones	MTM
"	20	-	Lewis Gun had cold.	MTM
"	21	-	No truck preparing 15 more guns	MTM
			Rations mor-	MTM

3rd Sheet 10TH Bde. 17 Div. Army Form C. 2118

WAR DIARY
or
INTELLIGENCE SUMMARY Oct 1916
(Erase heading not required.)

Instructions regarding War Diaries and Intelligence
Summaries are contained in F.S. Regs, Part II.
and the Staff Manual respectively. Title Pages
will be prepared in manuscript.

Place	Date	Hour	Summary of Events and Information	Remarks and references to Appendices
Trenche	22	7h	Moves from PMS. 15 Trench 4th Army Raided w Crater Top over Bump Trench by 33rd Division	
"	23	—	Trench 32.53. 69213. 48746. 21450 reconnoyed for artillery	RTW
"	24	—	Trench 32071 went 9 km get stores in trench 48273- met 10 tales mys horse	RTW
"	25	"	No trucks arrived. Roadie went	RTW
Citadel to 4 mmmel	26	"	Took over loving- Stores, abt 57 of 4th Brir Artillery	RTW
"	27	"	Trench 15842 horse scarce, a 3rd Brigade	RTW
"	28	"	Trench 5235 sent 4 ton truck collecting a 7771 sent 9 ton to truck unit, crocks - broke	RTW
"	29	"	Trench 20003 horse get clearer a forward company a beyond	RTW
"	30	"	" 37645 sent 25 wayn for kut trains arrange horse arrive evening in werely road	RTW
"	31	"	Trench 41374, 21611, 13116, + 15831 containing forward wants arriving	RTW

1875 Wt. W593/826 1,000,000 4/15 J.B.C. & A. A.D.S.S./Forms/C. 2118.

WAR DIARY
of
D.A.D.O.S. 17th Division
Nov: 1916.

Vol 16

WAR DIARY or INTELLIGENCE SUMMARY

Army Form C. 2118

57 R.F.S 17 Bn   November 1916 / Lt Colonel

Instructions regarding War Diaries and Intelligence Summaries are contained in F. S. Regs., Part II. and the Staff Manual respectively. Title Pages will be prepared in manuscript.

(Erase heading not required.)

Place	Date	Hour	Summary of Events and Information	Remarks and references to Appendices
Trones Post	1	—	Advance troops on Trones Post — Recce Troops on Trenches Advance orders for Raiders to be Emergency to Trenches in North recces count to lands at Advanced camp. Trench 1672 north 1654 trench Camps reconspts F.29 SW 1.m 17 R.i artillery	
	2		Trench 41374, 21.6.11, 13.16.63 appears as Raiders from enemy to blockage in Road Trones only with Buildings past Cellar 41.6.11.	
	3		Trench 14.7.53 + 21.80 trench hour Chou 10.18 p.c. coverage for NEW 65 Bee RJG Trench 24537	
	4		Trench 41374, 21.6.11, 13.16.63 now cleared. Also Trench 22633 c 15.3831	NEW NEW
	5		Trench 21.5.609 north 10 km. Trees ports shull di	NEW
	6		Point Trench 62.54.62 with 2 trans farm	NEW
	7		Trench 45837 could survive damaged by Germans, or Trench 9813 west vehicle	
	8		Trench 15.75.y north 12 m bridge Trench 23.916 south Cub Bking Now	NEW
	9			NEW

WAR DIARY
or
INTELLIGENCE SUMMARY

Army Form C. 2118

57728 17 Dn
Nayeympat 1916

Place	Date	Hour	Summary of Events and Information	Remarks and references to Appendices
Mennevel l.am	11		Trues 164434 escort to base Rec. clothing & 27214 well shot	HJW
	12		The knsh, two 2 Lewis Guns to S Scoff horsesom	HJW
	12		a musketeer in Pistol Tower	HJW
	13		Tower containing Chart & South reconnipt & new Railhead	HJW
	14		70417 more tour to TREOX. on recomying chart by Rail to new Railhead	HJW
OISSY	15		Moral camp to OISSY	HJW
"	16		Received the truck of recomyas	HJW
"	17		Trunk 579 west 19 which, troth excellent, ground sh	HJW
"	18		Trunk 5-131C west bet clothing Boot & Cardigan	HJW
"	19		Trunk 12323 went brown woollen	HJW
	20		No trains	
	21		Trunk 24454 west triges to Sweden anthong, a Lewis gun for Chauvenes	HJW

WAR DIARY or INTELLIGENCE SUMMARY

Army Form C. 2118.

2nd SK&K

To 7 ASC 17 DW

16 September 1916

(Erase heading not required.)

Instructions regarding War Diaries and Intelligence Summaries are contained in F.S. Regs., Part II. and the Staff Manual respectively. Title Pages will be prepared in manuscript.

Place	Date	Hour	Summary of Events and Information	Remarks and references to Appendices
DISSN	22		Tannak 1554 runt 7 tons hour short a sugar scotta	RYW
"	23		47015 & 20116 sent here clothing	RYW
"	24		49770 sent flannels	RYW
"	25		12004 & 16 tons of metal hurried on good stock	RYW
"	26		131651 - rehash	RYW
"	27		131757	RYW
"	28		No hours. Complete a writing one car on scrap grease appear to it made in clothing & trails, about more attache to say points to external	RYW
"	29		Tannak 200716 tank expansionals stores & wharves	RYW
"	30		Tannak 211045 recongropes store from 15 Dw	RYW

WAR DIARY or INTELLIGENCE SUMMARY

Army Form C. 2118

27ADOS 17th Div September 1916 for S/Sgt

Vol 17

Place	Date	Hour	Summary of Events and Information	Remarks and references to Appendices
OISSY	1		Trwer. 92398 indt vehicle	RTN
"	2		Trwper 234230 154110 indt pack clothing & boots from Rouen	RTN
			" 61113, 46777, 200738 indt vehicle held up 2 grows for reparation & grave clothes from tent	
			At present the troops in action numbering 60 km are reverts on one day, cannot grow in movement a painter it is impossible to clean stores. Men billeted in the abotte time 1-6 hours	
	3		Trwer 200715 indt 12 km of broken horse shoe & grew caps	RTN
	4		no truck. Routine work, & visits stores	
	5		no truck. Patient work	
	6		Trwr 92492 indt 68942 indt vehicle time 2	RTN
	7		Trwr 92492 & 15205 indt Tamper & Pants clothing repairs	RTN

WAR DIARY or INTELLIGENCE SUMMARY

Army Form C. 2118.

December 1916
7th Week

Place	Date	Hour	Summary of Events and Information	Remarks and references to Appendices
Oisey	8		Indent 8030. Boot Horseshoes. 8 Noses joysis Grate Chop Cutting Machine	F.K.
"	9		— Indent 59R23 Boot Clothing.	F.K.
"	10 M/o		553375 Indent General Stores	F.K.
"	13		To Lunel Rangot Rooking with Horses from Depot 8 Corner	F.K.
Corbie	14		Indent 1102. 1 Runny Ord Syrup, but taken LC. Conference with	F.K.
"			G.O.C.5. at Minutte re Exemples de Parisien	F.K.
"	15		Indent 21,600 5000 P.H. Helmets	F.K.
"			22213 Indent Horseshoes in Bales Blankets Pannier Stores.	F.K.
"	16		No Indent. Routine work.	F.K.
"	17		Indent 5750 Indent — Capt. Stratton. Clothing Boots anklle.	F.K.
"	19		43058 Kichn body, Water cart 10 wheel	F.K.
"	21		21003. Indent clothing etc.	F.K.
"	23		Postanes Indent. 1 Case tree tykt, 9 tree sparpark	F.K.
"			Indent 2700 Boot Drawers vest, Clothing	F.K.
"	—		— A. 2837 Indent ankle Socks	F.K.
"	24		— 10727 — 23 Green Timber of tunne Stoves workshops	F.K.
Motor	25		— 161027 — Batt Cape Socks Socks Drawers	F.K.

WAR DIARY
or
INTELLIGENCE SUMMARY
(Erase heading not required.)

Army Form C. 2118

December 1916.
3rd Sect.

Place	Date	Hour	Summary of Events and Information	Remarks and references to Appendices
Hindu Bet	27		Ind R 415'33. Indl Bot Anti F.S.	
—	29	14618	The Velus from 50th M.T. Coy. Ind horseshoes	F.I.
—	30	200965"	Ind clothing S.D.	F.I.
—	31	9912	18 cases 513 Boxes Carriers magazine/pen/run	F.I.
—	31	23567	9 Ton Ind General Stores.	F.I.

F. Shurjan
Capt OS IBn.

Karachi
HQ 17th Div

War diary for Jan
1917 herewith

30/1/17

Forwarded
DADOS
17th Div

WAR DIARY or **INTELLIGENCE SUMMARY**   Army Form C. 2118

D.A.D.O.S 17th Div.   January 1917

Place	Date	Hour	Summary of Events and Information	Remarks
Plateau	1st		Issue No. 152225 Issue Caps, Shirts, Socks, Drawers, Vests	
	2nd		2487 Running out of things, 1 pair Britches	
			885 Compris 5 in C.T. 1400 Blankets	
	3		72486 Issue, Boots, Shirts, Blankets	
	6		21008 Issue, Drawers, Vests Clothing S.D.	
			139/46 Issue Shirts Socks	
	7		60159 20 Running out of things	
			8804 17 stores issued half stores to units a.c.	
			11008 Hind Part bolts G.S. wagon, One spare Cart	
	8		164/46 Issue Cape Shirt Socks Gum boots Capeshee also	
			Sons 20th Div.	
			5566 Issue troth Brown	
	10/11		4955 27 Occu. Limbers Back 106 Tabs corn Pullovers	
			2991 S.D.	
	11		4471 S.D Regs Horse 174	
	12		2616 Issue Stockings, etc.	
			19456 13 Sheets Back Books Knitted + Picaric	
	13		26/267 Issue Clothing S.D. drawers Bootlaces	

D.A.D.O.S. 17th Div. January 1917
Army Form C. 2118.
2nd Sheet.

WAR DIARY
or
INTELLIGENCE SUMMARY
(Erase heading not required.)

Place	Date	Hour	Summary of Events and Information	Remarks and references to Appendices
Bottom Reviews.	14th 15th		Iuer R. 73088 Buck Pieces stores 13 bales blankets and 17 Reeles	
			17355 — Shirts, socks, drawers, brushes	
			8 Q.4328 via Acrescamps Rugstores lors	
			2421. 8 R.O. Springs 1 Curse Breech Sleeve (4 Seconds) 1 turn D Bout 18 RFA.	
	15"		Division moved to Corbie	
	16		Iuer 62770 Buck & bales blankets	
	17		P.S. 23931 1 Harres cart 2 wheeler R.O. Springs	
			Iuer 44381 1 Horse part, lent G.S. 1 wgn D. G.S.	
			2 9578 Buck Drawers	
			4 2523. — Shirts, Socks, Drawers.	
			2 6382 — Bubbins etc.	
	18		Sections 14 – 15	
			From the date inclusive all outstanding Indents for Ordnance were cancelled & items in arrears to be claimed again by fresh Indents. References for ordering from Division to Division. Divisional items being now entered by us wer Issues.	
			Iuer 25576 Buck Boric Shoes	
	19 20		20216 — Clothing L.B. Brown road.	
			14786 H.F. Cases S'Boots 19 k Shoes	

WAR DIARY or INTELLIGENCE SUMMARY

Army Form C. 2118.

D.A.D.O.S. 17th Div.   January 1917   3rd Sheet

Place	Date	Hour	Summary of Events and Information	Remarks and references to Appendices
Merieux	21		Rec'd 95896 Rue R Bandoliers & Steels	
"	22		2,04447 — Clothing	
"	23		4,18441 16 pdrs without B.M. & 81 Bdr	
"	24		6,13,10 14 R.O. Springs, 60 kite Batteries & Steels	
"	25		233,59 Rec'd Bombs &c 10 Cases bty Wheels, 3 Rear Pln. Wheels	
"	27		3,907 — Greatcoats, tops, clothing & drawers Rec'd RSD 337 hub. assy. Carthge ft	
Platoon	28		left Carter for Arrieurs	
"	29		Rec'd 7698. m.c. Case & .... Lyke Sue for 8 Batt. W. Rtr 1/mm fuse 15 MKIII	
"	30		88,22 Bush caps, Skins, Sock Saxon	
"	31		58,10 Studs, 65 pair Tubes, 20 R.O. Springs, Bush, win fur Magazine	
			902 — Bush hooks	

Vol 19

Confidential

War Diary

of

D.A.D.O.S. 17th Division

for

February 1917

Army Form C. 2118.

WAR DIARY
or
INTELLIGENCE SUMMARY
(Erase heading not required.)

D.A.D.O.S. 17ᵗʰ Div.　　February, 1917

Place	Date	Hour	Summary of Events and Information	Remarks and references to Appendices
Rahen.	1		Ind RR. 10086	5 steel Bath Hotin ed. 56 Cates Knive Utensils.	
	2		14/332	2 RO springs BuR Horseshoes.	
	4		50220	BuR Boots Clothing	
	5		3019	3" link rosies for 7 T.M.B. BuR Box respirator for stores in trenches	
	7		14/1055	BuR Bout Socks Drawers Caps Blankets	
	8		92641	— Rations 14/ Cases box respirator	
	10		2370 -	— Clothing SD vest, also lining for flora. (20 A. Dr.)	
	12		14/113	2 Vickers guns for 52 R.C. Bay. BuR box respirators	
	13		3947"	Camel seat sight for a Btt / 78 Bde. to ewi jun.	
	13		4495	Wa Roshas camps. 6. Regt. Mules	
	14		2057	BuR Capes Mac. Boots 340 Blankets.	
	15		55/203	18 Pdr. site B.M for A Btt / 7 Bde. BuR side Release Brushes &c.	
	16			Belt bolt. Buck 78 152243 including 26 wheels & RO forms. BuR fans dress indicator lights F.P. Railhead Changed to Plateau.	
Plateau.	17		7/79	BuR Capes Mac. Clothing S.D.	
	18			Railhead van Changed to "Plateau"	
	18		8077	the Lewis gun for 7 & Yorks	
	18		137/4	18 Pdr. (Anzonia) cannon for A Bde / 78 Bde. 1 Headpad under G.S. 907 for Horse case F.P.	
Meriaumont.	19			than, buccaneer adjatic + Palladium Changed to Meriaumont. Much 10/469."	
	19			7 Sleept. BuR Agents Stas Brilliance cases BuR respirator	
	20		10/335	Searchlight (7) 70th BuR Bandages acceliquant.	

Army Form C. 2118.

WAR DIARY
or
INTELLIGENCE SUMMARY

(Erase heading not required.)

D.A.D.O.S. 7th Div. 2nd Sheet

Instructions regarding War Diaries and Intelligence Summaries are contained in F. S. Regs., Part II. and the Staff Manual respectively. Title Pages will be prepared in manuscript.

Place	Date	Hour	Summary of Events and Information	Remarks and references to Appendices
Reserve	20		Sent R.R. AH/5 - 1 G.S. Wagon for 101 Coy Div Train and 2 wheelers 9 N Riding Regt. also 23 Packages in 20 A Div Ammt. P. 2002.41	
	21		Sent H.P. 210 S.AA. Sent kpt Clothing S.D.	
	22		9/19 118 Packages in clothing S.D 50 groups 2d Sheets Sent Pithoms etc	
	24		57/112. Sent Clothing S.D.	
	25		23409 6 Sheets 111 Machine Gun Clush Sent Horse shoes, knives etc	
	26		Here precaution withdrawn but Div Traffic Act Job resumed	
			93039 Div Sun from Div Reset.	
	27		70.78 85 Packs p number	

Kw57
Darby
7 Div

WAR DIARY or INTELLIGENCE SUMMARY

Army Form C. 2118.

March 1917

Place	Date	Hour	Summary of Events and Information	Remarks and references to Appendices
Rouen	1		Case R.O. 20005b 1 Case 1/A Level for 5th & 1/R Banty	
Rouen	3		210802 1 case zinc for 10" Shrapnel	
	4		40699 104 pieces Timber	
			33349 16 Sheets Steel Wrapper Saftin	
			222 Rolls oil B.P. wrappers for A Bd/G 79 Pdr. 14.5 cwt for 18 Pr. 9 Pdr	
	5		19990 11 Sheets R.O. Young	
	6		21499 12 Sheets	
	7		67147d Bulk few cases bookends "Clothing" drawers	
	8		15322 c 24 Stuts L.R. Raggin wires Steth CG 24 per jar	
	9		915 15" R9 Spm. B.P. R.L. Velvet, Lubukury	
			54311 1 Kitchen table top, 1 Bridge, 1 Hangard wed C.S. B. forms	
				1 water tank for 52 reed Highland & 2 kitchen tables for	
				12 R. Manch. Rs.	
	10		183 1 water tank for 10th R. Welsh & 2nd March Rs & Do	
				Kitchen dressing for 6th Dorset.	
			Orig of transport & packing on Tarmac to twice 6. Clatam to	
			Sinck and go floors, for the local vacume tube for soil	
Rouen & Chatam	15		15 for B.P. Clothing	
	1		200411 6 Black 6 Wagon frame heel steel	

WAR DIARY or INTELLIGENCE SUMMARY

Army Form C. 2118.

D.A.D.O.S. 17th Div.   2nd Sheet
March 1917.

Place	Date	Hour	Summary of Events and Information	Remarks and references to Appendices
Hn.-A.Uster	16		Issue R.P. 3747 5 Steel Rack Bar reservoirs, Nose bags etc.	A.K.
Programme	21		4131 + two Rifle Brackets	
	23		16801/3 4 ton Friend Lorr.	
			24574 7 - do -	
	24		36015 Wagons and G.S. 7/ pr. meters + 1 Water cart for 6th Dorset	
	25		55.105 General Servi.	
	26		15168 - do - Wheels	
	27		147 045 H.H. Sacks for Regt. Orderly	
	28		29513 L. ton Friend Lorrie	
	29		92040 9 - do - 7	
				1 15 pdr Am. Wagon + Regt. colours for R.A.M. (1st + 2nd R.E.)
	30		470405 General Stores	

Frank Richards
Capt
D.A.D.O.S
17th Div.

WAR DIARY or INTELLIGENCE SUMMARY

Army Form C. 2118

(Erase heading not required.)

DADOS 17 D
April 1917

Place	Date	Hour	Summary of Events and Information	Remarks and references to Appendices
LE CAUROY.	2		LIEUT G SHERRIFF arrived from 1 CORPS to take over duties of D.A.D.O.S. 17th Divison from LIEUT F BUTCHER A.O.D. evacuated to BASE sick.	21
			Truck No 6512. 9 tons general stores	
	7		" " 59440 1 Cart water tank for 7th Lincolns	
			Truck No 41609 12 tons clothing	
BERNEVILLE	8		Moved to BERNEVILLE.	
			Truck No 22496 5 tons clothing	
			" " 151481 including 25 wheels, horseshoes etc	
	10		Truck No 1506 Bulk stores also 15 cooks steel helmets & 8 cycles	
			" " 59902 wk R.S. RE wagon & 2 water carts	
	11		" " 50216 1 water cart.	
	12		" " 150880 including 14 wheels.	
	13		" " 146036 10 tons clothing.	
	14		" " 56343 including 12 wheels	
	15		" " 3534 including 11 wheels & bulk horseshoes	
			Moved to ARRAS.	

Army Form C. 2118.

WAR DIARY
or
INTELLIGENCE SUMMARY
(Erase heading not required.)

Instructions regarding War Diaries and Intelligence Summaries are contained in F. S. Regs, Part II. and the Staff Manual respectively. Title Pages will be prepared in manuscript.

Place	Date	Hour	Summary of Events and Information	Remarks and references to Appendices
ARRAS	16		Indent No 211044 with 4 wheels & old tail store	
	21		Wrote No 1802 including 35 ¼ btls or general store	
	22		" No 12229 R.Forms clothing	
	24		" No 4664 including 4 wheels, manufactures etc	
	25		Withdrew 1-18 pr gun & 1 4.5 gun carriage from Gun Park. Breeches & cranks	
			Wrote No's 25501 & 27746 with 15 ½ Clothing	
			Wrote No 54689 with 18 pr limber & amm wagon & 1 4.5 wagon limber	
	26		Moved to LE CAUROY	
			Very busy re-equipping the campaign after heavy fighting & difficulties again with heavy Gun & spare parts large amt.	
			Wrote No 2969 including 18 pr & 4.5 howitzers etc	
	27		- 1390 95 Gun tail slides	
	29		Received 32 heavy guns & 2 Vickers from 3rd Army Gun Park also sufficient	
	30		Clothing SD & Boots to re-equip the division	

11/5/17

P.Benny Lt.
D A D O S. 1/4 D S

WAR DIARY
or
INTELLIGENCE SUMMARY

Army Form C. 2118.

Diary 8 17 D
May 1917 Vol 22

Place	Date	Hour	Summary of Events and Information	Remarks and references to Appendices
LE CAUROY	1		Dump at No 13 Billet. A fine capacious dump with plenty of room for Office, armourers & bootmakers shop.	95
	4		After a few days rest the Division was sent forward again on reserve. On the night of the 4th/5th an ammunition dump situated near some billets went up & the billets caught fire instantly. The men had barely time to get out of them before the roofs made fall in. This resulted in a big loss of equipment of all kinds. We were able to replace losses in rifles, bayonets, equipment etc from Salvage collected from Salvage Dumps of I, VI, XIII & XVII Corps.	95
	6		11 Lewis Guns were received from 3rd Army Gun Park.	95
ARRAS	11		Units who had suffered in above mentioned fire were now ready to go into the line again fully equipped with fighting kit. Moved to ARRAS. 34 Rue des Augustines.	95 95

WAR DIARY or INTELLIGENCE SUMMARY

Army Form C. 2118.

Place	Date	Hour	Summary of Events and Information	Remarks and references to Appendices
ARRAS.			This dump is in a house which has not been very badly damaged by shell fire. The street is rather narrow for lorry traffic otherwise the dump is quite a useful one.	
	16		5 Lewis Guns & 1 Vickers received from Gun Park	
	18		4 Lewis Guns	"
	20		Lewis Guns & 1.18/per Gun	"
	22		1 3" Stokes Trench Mortar received from Gun Park	"
	28		1 Lewis Gun received from Gun Park	"
			During the month 133 Lewis Guns have been stripped, overhauled & repaired in the Divisional Armr Shop	"
	31		Moved back to COUTURELLE.	

A. Hewitt Lt
D.A.D.O.S. 17th Div

WAR DIARY
or
INTELLIGENCE SUMMARY

DADS - 17th Div Army Form C. 2118
June 1917

Vol 2

Place	Date	Hour	Summary of Events and Information	Remarks and references to Appendices
COUTURELLE	1		Very inefficient dump. Railroad SAULTY.	BS
	2		Wagon RE complete received from BASE	BS
			Very little refitting & re-equipping was necessary this time as had been able to supply units demands normally while they were in the line.	BS
			Great shortage of Service Colr Paint at the Base & all units were desirous of repainting their vehicles	BS
	18		Truck No 33121 with 2 Trench Mortar Handcarts & 1 Travelling Kitchen also truck No 32353 with a GS wagon.	BS
S⁺ NICOLAS	23		Moved to S⁺ NICOLAS, near ARRAS on this date & took over BS dump from 34th Div.	BS
			Dump is situated in a battered Oil Factory, very commodious with	BS

Army Form C. 2118.

WAR DIARY
or
INTELLIGENCE SUMMARY
June (contd) 1917
(Erase heading not required.)

Place	Date	Hour	Summary of Events and Information	Remarks and references to Appendices
St николая	30		with a very bad roof & most unpleasant odour, but is convenient being near D.H.Q. & transport lines. Railhead ARRAS. 9.45 Trench Mortar received.	

R Shand Lt Col
DADOS 1st K Div

1/7/17

Army Form C. 2118.

WAR DIARY
or
INTELLIGENCE SUMMARY

D.A.Q.G.S. July 1917
17th Division

(Erase heading not required.)

Vol 24

Place	Date	Hour	Summary of Events and Information	Remarks and references to Appendices
ST NICHOLAS	2		Railhead ARRAS. 1 Mess Cart - 1 Water Cart received.	
	4		Went to HAVRE with the A.A. Q.M.G. DA.Q.M.G. of the division with a view to visiting the various depots where they deal with salvage sent down from the front. The question of salvage is receiving very great attention at present.	
	9		Indented for a Vickers gun to replace one destroyed by shell fire.	
	16		Indented for one 18 pdr. Q.F. to replace one condemned for wear. Indent for 3 other 18pdr Q.F's are still outstanding	
	18		1 Water Cart received from Base	
	22		G.S. Wagon received.	

Army Form C. 2118.

WAR DIARY
or
INTELLIGENCE SUMMARY

July 1917 (Cont'd)

(Erase heading not required.)

Instructions regarding War Diaries and Intelligence Summaries are contained in F. S. Regs., Part II and the Staff Manual respectively. Title Pages will be prepared in manuscript.

Place	Date	Hour	Summary of Events and Information	Remarks and references to Appendices
S NICHOLAS	24		1 G S wagon & 1 hind part limbered GS wagon received from Base	
	27		1 Water cart & 2 French Motor handcarts received from Base	
	30		1 Travelling Kitchen Tandy & 1 Water Cart received from Base	
			This month has been a very quiet one. Supplies have come up very regularly	

3/8/17

[signature] Capt
DADOS 17 Div

2449 Wt. W14957/M90 750,000 1/16 J.B.C. & A. Forms/C.2118/12.

Army Form C. 2118.

WAR DIARY
or
INTELLIGENCE SUMMARY — AUGUST 1917.
(Erase heading not required.)

MRLNS "B" Sqn

Instructions regarding War Diaries and Intelligence Summaries are contained in F.S. Regs., Part II. and the Staff Manual respectively. Title Pages will be prepared in manuscript.

Place	Date	Hour	Summary of Events and Information	Remarks and references to Appendices
ST NICHOLAS	5		Received from Base 1 Water Cart, 1 Kitchen Body, 1 New Cart & 1 hind part Limit. G.S. Wagon	VM 25
	9		Received from Third Army Gun Park 1. 4.5 Q.F. Howitzer.	95
	10		Received from Base 1 Maltese Cart - 1 Water Cart	95
	11		Collected from Third Army Gun Park one long range 9.45 Mortar & issued to Heavy trench Mortar Bty.	95
	17		Received 21 bicycles to be distributed under new reorganization. Note: issued to exchange for horses also 1 limb G.S. Wagon	95
	18		Received from Base 1242 Water cans as first instalment to be issued to replace Petrol cans at present in use. Cans do not appear to be strong enough for purpose required	95

2449 Wt. W14957/Mg0 750,000 1/16 J.B.C. & A. Forms/C.2118/12.

Army Form C. 2118.

WAR DIARY
or
INTELLIGENCE SUMMARY — AUGUST 1917
(Erase heading not required.)

Instructions regarding War Diaries and Intelligence Summaries are contained in F. S. Regs., Part II. and the Staff Manual respectively. Title Pages will be prepared in manuscript.

Place	Date	Hour	Summary of Events and Information	Remarks and references to Appendices
ST NICHOLAS	19		3" Stokes Mortar received from Base	
	25		2 Common Handcarts + 1 Motorcart received.	
	27		Received from Base 1 Water Cart, 1 Kitchen Body, 3 men cook + 1 G.S. Wagon	
	31		Received from Base 1 Mens Cart + 1 Kitchen RE Wagon + 1 forget Limber G S Wagon.	
			The month has been very wet + stormy + considerable difficulty has been experienced in keeping stores dry + any.	

Signed Capt
DADOS 4 Div

WAR DIARY
or
INTELLIGENCE SUMMARY

(Erase heading not required.)

Army Form C. 2118.

Place	Date	Hour	Summary of Events and Information	Remarks and references to Appendices
St Michaels	13		Received from Dirce 2 Turret Mantlets 3" Stokes	
	14		Received from Dirce 1 Travel Anton 3" Stokes	
	20		Received 1 Water Cart - 1 Limber A.S. Wagon	
	21		1 Travel Anton 3" Stokes received	
	24		Raid at AGNEZ-LÈS-DUISANS	
			1 Travelling Kitchen Body (fore part limber) received	
			Moved to L.E. CAUROY.	
LeCauroy	26		Railhead FREVENT.	
	28		Collected 1 Vickers M.G from 3rd Army Gun Park	
			Collected 1 Lewis gun " " " "	
			Received 1 Travel Anton 3" Stokes	

DADOS 17 Div

WAR DIARY
or
INTELLIGENCE SUMMARY

Army Form C. 2118.

2nd A.T.S / 7
October 1914

Place	Date	Hour	Summary of Events and Information	Remarks and references to Appendices
Le Cavroy	3		Railroad PROVEN. Reorganised 3 trucks to PROVEN. Leave all stores & most of personnel at MONDICOURT & move great B.	VA 27
	4		Moved to PROVEN.	do
PROVEN.	5		Fairly good turn-out dump. Details down in WATOU Road.	do
			Day clearing etc. (in reorganised trucks containing Park)	
			Chargeup for winter issue.	
	9		2 Vickers Machine Guns received from Zer Park	do
	12		Moved to ELVERDINGHE.	do
			5 Two Nissen Huts for officers & solfa. Dumb body found for traffic.	do
ELVERDINGHE	13			do
	15		Received 2 lewis guns from Zer Park	do

WAR DIARY or INTELLIGENCE SUMMARY

Army Form C. 2118.

October 1917

Place	Date	Hour	Summary of Events and Information	Remarks and references to Appendices
ELVERDINGHE	16		1 Stokes 3" Trench Mortars & 8 Lewis Guns received from Gun Park	
	17		Received 2 Vickers MG from Gun Park	
			Moved back to PROVEN	
	18		2 Truck loads of Gun Parts Lkits received from Base	
			2 Lewis Guns received from Gun Park	
	20		Transferred Broad Artyk 50th Div s/left a Sgt, a Storeman & lorry with them. Sent 2 truck loads of parts to WATTEN & moved to	
ZUTKERQUE			ZUTKERQUE.	
			Took over offices & dump from 58 D. S. Park good but on various road	
	23		Leaders Jenkins & Waratoos & two received from Base	
	26		Collected 4 Lewis & 1 Vickers gun from Gun Park	
	29		Collected 2 Lewis Guns from Gun Park	
			Visited CALAIS Base	

B. Hunt Capt
3/11/17
DADOS 17 K 2 WS.

Army Form C. 2118.

WAR DIARY
or
INTELLIGENCE SUMMARY

(Erase heading not required.)

Range 17 D
NOVEMBER 1917

Place	Date	Hour	Summary of Events and Information	Remarks and references to Appendices
ZUTKERQUE	5		Railhead WATTEN. 1 Truck of Bot & FS received	
ELVERDINGHE	8		Moved to ELVERDINGHE Railhead B International Corner 2 Lorries received from Zero Park	
	11		Railhead ELVERDINGHE. 6 Trucks of Blankets received	
	14		1 Lorry Gen received from Zero Park	
	19.		2 Travelling Kitchens + 1 Aeroplane GS Lorries received from Base	
	20		2 Cars Water tank received from Base	
	23		1 Lorry Gen received from Zero Park 2 Cars Water Tanks & 2 Travelling Kitchens Lorries & 1 Aeroplane GS Lorries received from Base	

Army Form C. 2118.

WAR DIARY
or
INTELLIGENCE SUMMARY
(Erase heading not required.)

NOVEMBER 194/

Place	Date	Hour	Summary of Events and Information	Remarks and references to Appendices
ELVERDINGHE	24		2 Travelling Kitchens received from Base	£
	27		1 Vickers Gun received from Gun Park	£
	29		1 Lewis & 1 Vickers Gun received from Gun Park	£

Bewoy Capt
DADOS 4 Div

WAR DIARY
or
INTELLIGENCE SUMMARY

Army Form C. 2118.

DECEMBER 1917

WA 29

Place	Date	Hour	Summary of Events and Information	Remarks and references to Appendices
ELVERDINGHE	4	DADOS Mc Dury	One Vickers Gun received from Gun Park	S/S
	8		Moved to ZUTKERQUE. RAILHEAD. WATTEN.	S/S
ZUTKERQUE	11		One Vickers Gun received from Gun Park	S/S
	12		3 Bodies Travelling Kitchen received from Base	S/S
	14th		Sent stores off by rail & moved by lorry to ACHIET-LE-PETIT.	S/S
ACHIET-LE PETIT			RAILHEAD. BAPAUME. Very bad dump. Formed an emergency dump at BAPAUME	S/S
	19th		Moved to BEALENCOURT RAILHEAD BAPAUME	S/S
BEALENCOURT	20th		1 Body Travelling Kitchen & 5 French Motor Cart received from Base	S/S
	24th		Moved to Bus. RAILHEAD ROCQUIGNY.	S/S

WAR DIARY
or
INTELLIGENCE SUMMARY

(Erase heading not required.)

Army Form C. 2118.

Instructions regarding War Diaries and Intelligence Summaries are contained in F. S. Regs., Part II. and the Staff Manual respectively. Title Pages will be prepared in manuscript.

Place	Date	Hour	Summary of Events and Information	Remarks and references to Appendices
BUS.	25		Pontoon Bipartite for field (2RE received from Base. Pitched a marquee at railhead so as to be able to form a dump here in case of sudden thaw.	DS
	30		4 Water carts, 2 Forepart + 1 Hindpart limber G.S. Wagons. 1 RE limber Wagon + 1 maro cart received from Base.	DS
			On account of changing from Northern to Southern Base. supplies have not been coming up very regularly this month + on account of the hard frost it has been difficult to supply Horse Transport + Artillery with all the Front Coys. Nails necessary to enable them to move	DS

3/1/18

Shen/ Capt
DADGS 1/5 Div

WAR DIARY
or
INTELLIGENCE SUMMARY

Army Form C. 2118.

(Erase heading not required.)

January 1918   DADOS/5/17/2

Place	Date	Hour	Summary of Events and Information	Remarks and references to Appendices
B.V.S	1	DADOS 17th River	One Travelling Kitchen & 1 Water Cart received from Base	
	2		One Vickers Gun received from Advanced Gun Park	
	4		One Vickers Gun " " " "	
	6		One R.E. Limbered Wagon Body & 1 G.S. Wagon received from Base	
	10		2 18/pdr Q.F. Guns drawn from Advanced Gun Park to replace 2 k/u sent to Base for relining	
			2 Limo Guns received from Gun Park to replace 2 captured	
	20		1 Pontoon received from Base	
	27		One Vickers Gun received from Gun Park " " " "	
	31		2 18/pdr Q.F. Guns " " " " to replace 2 k/u sent to Base for relining	

The month has been a very quiet one. A certain amount of inconvenience was caused while "thaws" precautions were on, as horse transport had to be resorted to.

Shrint Col DADOS 17th Div

WAR DIARY
or
INTELLIGENCE SUMMARY   FEBRUARY 1918

Army Form C. 2118.

Place	Date	Hour	Summary of Events and Information	Remarks and references to Appendices
BUS			Routhead ROCQUIGNY.	
	2		1 Vickers M.G. drawn from Advanced Gun Park	
	3		1 Water Cart received from Base	
	6		1 18 Pr QF gun drawn from Advanced Gun Park & handed to 10 M	
			1 Vickers M.G. " " " "	
	12		1 Travelling Kitchen Body, 1 Water Cart + 1 G.S. Wagon received from Base	
	13		1 Vickers M.G. drawn from Advanced Gun Park	
	17		1 Vickers M.G. " " "	
	21		1 " "	
	22		1 6" Newton Trench Mortar received from Base	
			1 Trench Mortar Landcart, 1 L.G.S Wagon, 1 Water Cart + 1 Kitchen Body	
			received from Base	
	24		Moved K. BERTINCOURT.	

WAR DIARY or INTELLIGENCE SUMMARY

Army Form C. 2118.

Place	Date	Hour	Summary of Events and Information	Remarks and references to Appendices
BERTINCOURT	26		Railhead FREMICOURT. 1 Lewis gun drawn from Advanced Gun Park	
	28		1. 18pr QF gun & carriage drawn from " "	
			This month has been a very busy one owing to the re-organize[ation] of Divisions forming the Machine Gun Battalions, Introducing Battalion & Divisional forming the Machine Gun Battalions, Introducing Battalion	

Blank Capt
DADOS 17 Div
7/3/18

Army Form C. 2118.

WAR DIARY
or
INTELLIGENCE SUMMARY

(Erase heading not required.)

March 1918.

DWFS/17/A

Place	Date	Hour	Summary of Events and Information	Remarks and references to Appendices
BERTINCOURT	17			
			1. Vickers Gun received from Gun Park	V.G. 32
	15		1. 18ph Gun + 1. 18ph Carriage received.	
	21		German offensive opened.	
			Ammunition back to BEAULEN COURT.	
BEAULENCOURT	22		Mvd Office + started moving stores back to COURCELETTE	
	23		Owing to congestion on the roads were not able to get all stores away. At dawn 24th were forced to abandon about 3 lorry loads of stores at BEAULEN COURT.	
COURCELETTE	24		Army moved stores + Office to HENENCOURT but owing to flanking movement, having no transport available were forced to leave my Armourers, Shoemakers + Tailors tools behind.	
HENENCOURT	25		Moved to VARDENCOURT.	
VARDENCOURT	26		32 Vickers Guns received + issued.	
			35 Lewis Guns " "	

Army Form C. 2118.

WAR DIARY
or
INTELLIGENCE SUMMARY

(Erase heading not required.)

Place	Date	Hour	Summary of Events and Information	Remarks and references to Appendices
VARDENCOURT	26		Moved to PUCHVILLERS in the evening.	JS
PUCHVILLERS	27		Cleared JS	JS
	28		30 Lewis Guns delivered & issued.	JS
	29		Moved to MIRVAUX.	JS
MIRVAUX	30		12 Lewis Guns received.	JS
	31st		Moved Officer-dump to PIERRE GOT.	JS

Brey Capt
DADOS 1/Div

Army Form C. 2118.

WAR DIARY
or
INTELLIGENCE SUMMARY. APRIL 1918
(Erase heading not required.)

WO 95/17?

Place	Date	Hour	Summary of Events and Information	Remarks and references to Appendices
PERREGOT	4th		Railhead ROSEL	
	3		Moved to HAVERNAS	
HAVERNAS	5		12 Lewis Guns received from Gun Park	
	7		6 " " " " "	
	9		1 Stokes Mortar 3" received from Gun Park	
	12		20 Lewis Guns received	
			Moved to HALLOY-L-PERNOIS	
HALLOY	15		RAILHEAD. BELLE-ÉGLISE.	
			5 Lewis Guns Received for Div Arty from Gun Park	
			8 Trench Mortar Hand carts received from Base	
	16		36 Lewis Guns received from Gun Park	
			(Contd. DDOS 3rd Army ZB 663 dd 15/4/18)	
			Initial increase of other Bns.	

WAR DIARY
INTELLIGENCE SUMMARY

Army Form C. 2118.

Place	Date	Hour	Summary of Events and Information	Remarks and references to Appendices
HALLOY	1/6		394. Bel S Amm. for Vickers received from Gun Park, increasing scale from 18 to 24 per gun.	
	23		2 6" Mortar Trench Mortars received from Gun Park	
			6 Lewis Guns received from Gun Park	
	24		1 " " " "	
	25		½ Stokes Mortar 3" " "	
	28		4 Lewis Guns " "	
			1 " Vickers Gun " "	
	29		4 Lewis Guns " " as first supply in reserve	
			increase of Guns in charge of Pioneer Bn.	
			The heavy demands made on Base during this month to replace losses sustained during recent operations have been most admirably met.	

Signed / Capt. DADOS 17 Div.

WAR DIARY
or
INTELLIGENCE SUMMARY
(Erase heading not required.)

Army Form C. 2118.

MAY 1918

Place	Date	Hour	Summary of Events and Information	Remarks and references to Appendices
HALLOY-L- PERNOIS	7		Railhead ROSEL. # Lorries Iurus issued to Pioneer Bn as a first supply to bring their establishment up to 6 D.L.G's	
	13		1. Workshop Lorry received from Line Park as first supply to 4th M.T. Coy for Anti Aircraft purposes	
	19		Moved to RAINCHEVAL. Billet N°1. Road metalled courtyard for horse transport & full in to load, with good metalled courtyard for horse transport & full into	
RAINCHEVAL	25		Rejoined by Armourers who had been working forward at PUCHVILLERS reloading Machine Guns while dump was in back area RAILHEAD. BELLE. EGLISE.	
	26		1. Potato Iurus & Carriage drawn from Line Park	

WAR DIARY
INTELLIGENCE SUMMARY

Army Form C. 2118.

MAY 1918

Place	Date	Hour	Summary of Events and Information	Remarks and references to Appendices
RAINCKEVAL	28		36 Lewis Guns drawn from Fim Park. 4 for each Infantry Bn. This brings Bns up to Scale E. i.e. 24 LGs each exclusive of 4 for R.A.M.R. This month has on the whole been a very quiet one. Stores have been coming up with great regularity.	

Bland Capt
DADOS. 1st Div.

WAR DIARY
or
INTELLIGENCE SUMMARY

(Erase heading not required.)

JUNE 1918.

Place	Date	Hour	Summary of Events and Information	Remarks and references to Appendices
RAON CHEVAL			RAILHEAD. ROSEL.	
	2		1 Lewis Gun + 1 Stokes received from Gun Park.	
	4		1 Lewis Gun received + 1 18pdr Gun for A/79 drawn from Gun Park	
	6		1 18pdr Gun + Carr. drawn from Gun Park by B/79.	
	9		1 18pdr Gun + Carr. for B/79 + 1. 18pdr Carr. for C/79 drawn from Gun Park.	
	12		3 Lewis + 1 Vickers guns received from Gun Park.	
	13		1. 3" Stokes Trench Mortars received + 1. 4.5 Hows. drawn from Gun Park by D/79.	
	17		1. 3" Stokes Trench Mortar received from Gun Park.	
	19		1 Vickers Gun received + 1. 18pdr Gun drawn from Gun Park by B/79	

WAR DIARY
or
INTELLIGENCE SUMMARY

(Erase heading not required.)

Army Form C. 2118.

JUNE 1918

Place	Date	Hour	Summary of Events and Information	Remarks and references to Appendices
Ramleh (Cont.)	20		36 Lewis Guns received from Gun Park to replace nearly	
			as many. Shortage below up to Scale F. say 28 L.G.s each	
			according to Str.[?] A.A. work.	
	21		1 Motor Car received	
	22		1 Piper Car. drawn from Gun Park by 3/13.	
			1 Motor Car received " " "	
	23		1 4.5 How drawn " " " by DAM	
			This month have been a comparatively one otherwise	
			from coming up regular.	
			[signature] Major	
			D.A.D.O.S.	

Army Form C. 2118.

WAR DIARY
or
INTELLIGENCE SUMMARY
(Erase heading not required.)

JULY 1918

DADOS 17D

Instructions regarding War Diaries and Intelligence Summaries are contained in F. S. Regs., Part II. and the Staff Manual respectively. Title Pages will be prepared in manuscript.

Places	Date	Hour	Summary of Events and Information	Remarks and references to Appendices
RAINCHEVAL			RAILHEAD, ROSEL.	
	3		1 Vickers Gun received from Gun Park	25/5/31
	7		"	25/5/31
	10		36 Lewis Guns received from Gun Park & 1 Gun to Infantry Bde	25/5/31
			This brings them up to scale & viz 32 per Bn exclusive of	
			4 A.A. L.G's	
	12		1 Vickers Gun received from Gun Park & issued to M.G. Bn. for training	25/5/31
			purposes	
	13		1. 18 pdr Q.F. received from Gun Park	25/5/31
			1. 18 pdr Q.F. " " "	25/5/31
	19		1. Lewis Gun " " "	25/5/31
	21		12 " " " " for issue to Field Co RE.	25/5/31
			1. 18 pdr Q.F	25/5/31

WAR DIARY
or
INTELLIGENCE SUMMARY

Army Form C. 2118.

Place	Date	Hour	Summary of Events and Information	Remarks and references to Appendices
RANCHEIN	23		1. 3" Stokes Trench Mortar received from Gun Park	
	24		1 Actn OP. received from Gun Park	28/1
	25	16	Lewis Guns " " for issue to RFA Batteries	
			for A.A. purposes this brings them up to 4 per Bty	25/1 26/1
			1 3" Stokes Trench Mortar received from Gun Park	28/1
	30		1 4.3 How. received from Gun Park	
	31		1 Vickers Gun " " "	
			This month has been a very quiet one & supplies have been very regular.	

Benny Major
DADOS 17 Div.

WAR DIARY or INTELLIGENCE SUMMARY

Army Form C. 2118.

WO95/8772

August 1918

Vol 37

Place	Date	Hour	Summary of Events and Information	Remarks and references to Appendices
RAINNEVAL	1		RAILHEAD. ROSEL.	
			1. 18pdr QF. issued to A/49 Bde RFA	PS
			1 Lewis Gun received from Gun Park	PS
	2		1 18pdr QF. issued to C/79 Bde RFA.	PS
	3		1 Lewis Gun received from Gun Park.	PS
	4		3 Lewis Guns " " " "	PS
	5		1 " " " " as direct supply to D.A.C.	PS
	8		1 " " " "	PS
	10*		1 18pdr QF issued to C/79 Bde RFA.	PS
	13.		Moved to ALLONVILLE attached Anzac Corps IV Army	PS
			Moved to CORBIE (LA NEUVILLE)	PS
LA NEUVILLE	15		RAILHEAD. CORBE	PS
			1 Lewis Gun drawn from Gun Park	PS
	18*		Moved to PUCHEVILLERS returning to I Corps Third Army	PS

Army Form C. 2118.

WAR DIARY
or
INTELLIGENCE SUMMARY AUGUST 1918

(Erase heading not required.)

Instructions regarding War Diaries and Intelligence Summaries are contained in F. S. Regs., Part II. and the Staff Manual respectively. Title Pages will be prepared in manuscript.

Place	Date	Hour	Summary of Events and Information	Remarks and references to Appendices
PUCHEVILLERS	19		1 Vickers Gun + 3 Lewis Guns received from Gun Park	
	25		1 18/pr QF forwarded to Ordnance RFA	
			2 - 4.5" Hows issued to DAC 170th RFA	
			1 Vickers Gun received from Gun Park	
	26		1 Lewis Gun + 2 Vickers	
	27		Arrival 6 ENGLEBELMER	
			2 Vickers Guns received from Gun Park	
ENGLEBELMER	28		1 Lewis Gun received	
	29		1 Vickers Gun "	
	30		30 Lewis Guns "	
	31		19 " "	

B.H. Alyn
DADOS 17 Div

WAR DIARY or INTELLIGENCE SUMMARY

Army Form C. 2118.

SEPTEMBER 1916
111 Bde 14th Div

Place	Date	Hour	Summary of Events and Information	Remarks and references to Appendices
ENGLE BELMER	2		3 Lewis Guns issued to 7th Yorks	
	3		Moved to MARTINPUICH	
MARTINPUICH	6		1 Lewis Gun issued to 9th West Riding Regt	
	7		Moved to Le TRANSLOY	
			5 Lewis Guns issued to 10th Yorks Fus.	
Le TRANSLOY	8		1 Lewis Gun issued to 7th Lincolns 1 to 9th Borders	
	12		1 Vickers Gun issued to 11th M.G. Bn	
	13		2 Vickers Guns " " "	
	14		4 Lewis Guns issued to 10th West York, 18 to 12th Manchesters	
			6 to 10th Lancs Fus "	
	20		1 Lewis Gun issued to 9th W Riding Regt. 1 to 10 West Yorks	
			1 Vickers " " " M.G.C	
	21		1 3" Stokes Mortar issued to 50th Trench Mortar Bty.	

WAR DIARY
or
INTELLIGENCE SUMMARY

Army Form C. 2118.

SEPTEMBER 1918

Place	Date	Hour	Summary of Events and Information	Remarks and references to Appendices
LE TRANSLOY	20		2 Lewis Guns handed to 9th W. Riding Regt. 4 to 6th Drakes 4 to 10th W[ ]/pdo	
	21		3.5 yk East pdo 1 Lewis gun to 17 M.G.B.	
			3 Lewis Guns handed to 17th MGB	
			12 Lewis Guns handed to the brigade 3.5 yk Lewis the 10th [ ]	
	24		freeing 16 yk West Pontoons 1 Lewis Gun to 6 17th MG Coy 3 E 10 W pdo	
			1 Lewis gun 2 yk East pdo	
	27		1 Lewis Gun handed to 10 Lewis gun yk Pontoons	
	28			
	30		Moved to Fins	

DADOS M Div

WAR DIARY
or
INTELLIGENCE SUMMARY

Army Form C. 2118.

OCTOBER 1918

2nd Corps 17th Army

MM 39

Place	Date	Hour	Summary of Events and Information	Remarks and references to Appendices
FINS	1		4 Lewis Guns issued to 4th Jäger Regt	
	3		3 Vickers Guns " 1st M.G. Dn	
	11		Moved to Guillemin Farm between Warneton - Egnes	
	12		Moved to Montigny	
MONTIGNY	14		1 Vickers gun issued to 17th M.G. Bn	
			7 Lewis Guns " 1st Eastjske - 8 to 6th Drag	
	15		6 Vickers Guns " 17th M.G. B?	
			2 3" Stokes Trench Mortars " 50th Trench Mortar B?	
			25 " " "	
	18		14 Lewis guns issued to 12th Musketeers Regt, 15 to 10 Lewis Two	
			1 3" Stokes Mortars issued to 50th Trench Mor B?	
	19		13 Lewis guns issued to 9th Westphalian Hy Cav R Bat?	

Army Form C. 2118.

WAR DIARY
or
INTELLIGENCE SUMMARY

(Erase heading not required.)

OCTOBER 1918

Place	Date	Hour	Summary of Events and Information	Remarks and references to Appendices
MONTIGNY.	20		1 Lewis gun issued to 19th Field Coy RE	
	21		1 Vickers gun " " 17th MG Bn	
	22		Moved to INCHY.	
INCHY.	25		1 Spstka M.G. issued to 50th G Trench M.Bty 75	
	26		5 Lewis guns issued to 7th Division 4 to 7th Battns	

B. Walker
DADOS 17th Div.

WAR DIARY or **INTELLIGENCE SUMMARY**

Army Form C. 2118.

NOVEMBER 1918

Place	Date	Hour	Summary of Events and Information	Remarks and references to Appendices
INCHY.	5		Moved to POIX-DU-NORD	
POIX-DU-NORD	6		4 Lewis Guns moved to 1st Border Regt. - 2 to 10th Sherwood Foresters	
	7		Moved to LOCQUIGNOL (FORÊT DE MORMAL)	
LOCQUIGNOL	9		1 Vickers Gun moved to 17th Machine Gun Btn	
			1 18pdr Gun moved to B/149 Bde RFA	
	10		1 18pdr Gun moved to A/78 Bde RFA	
			5 Lewis Guns moved to 9th West Riding Regt - 5 to 12th Manchester Regt.	
	11		Hostilities ceased as from 11 o'clock.	
			1 Vickers Gun moved to 17th Machine Gun Btn	
			1 Lewis Gun moved to 10th West Yorks Regt - 2 to 10th Sherwood Foresters	
	12		Moved back to rest at INCHY.	
INCHY	13		1 18pdr gun moved to B/148 Bde RFA.	

Army Form C. 2118.

WAR DIARY
or
INTELLIGENCE SUMMARY
(Erase heading not required.)

NOVEMBER 1918

Place	Date	Hour	Summary of Events and Information	Remarks and references to Appendices
INCHY.	15		3" Stokes Mortar issued to 51st Trench Mortar By. Hostilities having ceased this remainder of the month was spent in refitting.	15

(Signed) Flynn
D.A.D.O.S. 17th Div.

Army Form C. 2118.

WAR DIARY
or
INTELLIGENCE SUMMARY
(Erase heading not required.)

DECEMBER 1918

Vol 4 1

Place	Date	Hour	Summary of Events and Information	Remarks and references to Appendices
INCHY	10		Moved back to HALLENCOURT	
HALLENCOURT			RAILHEAD. LONGPRE	
			At the beginning of the month considerable difficulty was experienced in receiving stores regularly from Base owing to shortage of Trucks.	
			At the end of the month all indents for ROUEN & HAVRE were transferred to CALAIS, on which Depot we are now based.	
			During the month Major G. SHERRIFF D.A.D.O.S. was acting A.D.O.S. at I Corps HQrs	

Blant Major
DADOS 4 Div

WAR DIARY or INTELLIGENCE SUMMARY

Army Form C. 2118.

Place: DAOURS
Month: JANUARY 1919

Place	Date	Hour	Summary of Events and Information	Remarks and references to Appendices
FRANVILLERS	15		Indent to Base for 2 Officers for 3/155 R.F.A. See Endorsee 7155 } Endurance for storing	2159
	16		" " " " 1 " " C/155 AFA B.C. " 2484	" " "
			" " " " 1 " " A/55 AFA Bde " 7361	" " the total
	20		" " " " 1 " " A/79 Bde RFA " 3595	" " arriving 25
	21		" " " " 2 " " A/79 Bde RFA " 7599 }	" " " 25
				7390 }	" " transport
	24		" " " " 1 " " C/79 Bde RFA " 4096	" " left

None of the guns are yet to hand. There has been a very serious shortage to the motor lorries of late and also of quilters during the month.

[signed]

WAR DIARY or INTELLIGENCE SUMMARY

Army Form C. 2118.

D.A.D.O.S
17th Division

February 1919

Place	Date	Hour	Summary of Events and Information	Remarks and references to Appendices
HALLENCOURT	1		1 Gun 18 QF. 4.5" Hows received from Base for D/78 Bde RFA	
			Rode to Base for 1 18pdr QF for C/78 Bde RFA to Allow S/B Gunners to train	
	7		" " " " " B/63 + A3me "	
	8		" " " " " B/49 Bde RFA	
			Lewis Guns received from Base for C/49 Bde RFA	
	12		" " " " " B/49 Bde RFA	

DADOS 17 Div

www.ingramcontent.com/pod-product-compliance
Lightning Source LLC
Chambersburg PA
CBHW081427160426
43193CB00013B/2216